MW00773436

1· August 2019

for Chelsea.

How They DECORATED

130 N. Bloodworth

[signature]

How They
DECORATED

Inspiration from Great Women of the Twentieth Century

P. GAYE TAPP

Foreword by

CHARLOTTE MOSS

RIZZOLI
NEW YORK

New York Paris London Milan

Contents

FOREWORD by Charlotte Moss   6

INTRODUCTION   9

Legacy STYLE

Lady Diana Cooper   17

Evangeline Bruce   31

Louise de Vilmorin   43

Sybil Connolly   53

In the Grand MANNER

Hélène Rochas   67

Gabrielle van Zuylen   81

Mona von Bismarck   93

Pauline de Rothschild   105

Fashionably CHIC

Babe Paley   121

Elsa Schiaparelli   135

Fleur Cowles   147

Pauline Trigère   157

Unconventional EYE

Bunny Mellon   171

Dominique de Menil   185

Georgia O'Keeffe   199

Lesley Blanch   209

BIBLIOGRAPHY   218

IMAGE CREDITS   222

ACKNOWLEDGMENTS   223

DEDICATION   224

FOREWORD

by Charlotte Moss

MADAME DE POMPADOUR WANTED A PLACE FOR PRIVACY SANS
the display and intrigue of Louis XV's court. It was her private hideaway—a boudoir, a
place designed for seclusion, personal pleasure, and amusement—that I have always
felt was somehow the beginning of a woman's independence at home. To be able
to define a space in square feet, then to furnish and decorate it according to one's
personal taste, is a form of expression that we take for granted today.

How They Decorated is an invitation to enter the enchanting worlds of sixteen
women—to experience their circles of influence and the results of their time spent
at the altar of elegance, comfort, and beauty. Sybarites and weavers of dreams, they
speak a common language. Each, in her own way, has been in a forensic pursuit of her
own definition of beauty. Lucky for us, so much of their quests for living in a state of
perpetual allure has been documented in images and words. In How They Decorated
Gaye Tapp promises a volume that will be constantly referred to—a must-have for
every library of style and design, and one that will show its own signs of love from
constant use over time.

Like sixteen novelettes, these women's stories are bound by a similar narrative—
one of loyalty, tenacity, generosity, hospitality, and so much more. There is a thin
red thread that connects each woman between these covers. I am not talking about
similarities in style, but undeniable commonalities in terms of character between all
of these diverse personalities. A strong identity, a distinct point of view, a sense of
humor—some wicked, some reckless, some drier than a perfect martini (shaken not
stirred)—as well as determination, discipline, and drive. An inner beauty manifested
in an outward appearance, whether the decoration of houses or the manner of
entertaining, whether gardens, collections, or an aura felt long after she has left the
room. And their own personal brands of *je ne sais quoi*: the indefinable, coveted,

"name your price, sorry not for sale" quality that most people call *style* yet is actually elegance, rarer than rare.

True elegance never swims with the tide; it never follows fashion. Elegance surveys current styles, carefully selects, and adapts, leaving no trace of a trend or a must-have of the season, like the vanishing vapor trail of a jet plane. This innate capacity—to mix the unmatched, to create a look that cannot be broken down to the sum of its parts, to produce an illusion or a reality that is inimitable (because it is original)—can never, ever be faked.

Please, let's not forget the pleasure derived from all of these pursuits: A favorite menu that consistently proved to be a pleaser. The garden design that enhanced not only the life of the gardener but also the lives of everyone who visited. The wardrobe that surprised and excited, whether by the presence of magnificent jewels or by finds from the souk that were paired with vintage couture or caftans and shawls.

Once inside your nest, what does a visitor see, touch, feel, and smell? When he or she leaves, what resonates? It is in our nature to put a stamp on our surroundings, to leave an imprint of our personality on our rooms and our houses. When this process has been imbued with heart, soul, and emotion—with what is personal, with the true spirit and DNA of the inhabitant—the resulting creation exudes a joie de vivre that gives joy in its lifetime and sometimes long after. Such is the case with the rooms within these covers, rooms many of you have long committed to memory for the sincerity of their style and for an indescribable atmosphere—that mystical aura that holds you, trancelike, every time you open the book or return to the timeworn, yellow-edged pages of your clippings files. And if given a test, you would pass with flying colors because you can draw the floor plan; describe the color scheme; and remember specific fabrics, the pattern of a painted floor, art on the walls, and the iconic objects that reside on a certain bouillotte table.

Whether exotic, urbane, cerebral, literary, or social, each of the subjects in *How They Decorated* moved to the beat of her own drum; yet their lives have all stirred our own in some way. There is no single formula. There is no single style. Each had her own creative intensity, her joy for life—some an unabashed delight with fashion, others a unique personal style laced with an unapologetic sans souci bohemianism, and still others a razor-sharp focus to achieve perfection. And then, there were the rarest of birds: those who knew that perfection was in the imperfect, that the unconventional was simply using conventional things unconventionally.

These women made us think then; they make us think now. Thank God for them all.

INTRODUCTION

"Decorating is autobiography."

–GLORIA VANDERBILT

THERE ARE MANY CELEBRATED WOMEN WHO LIVED WITH GREAT style but are lost to the pages of old magazines or books, waiting to be rediscovered. Portraits of these women by great artists of the day remain; they gaze out at us, framed by their beautiful rooms. Most of those interiors are gone. Yet the portraits remain, luring us to discover more about how they decorated.

How They Decorated revives and revisits the beloved rooms I was introduced to as a child sitting cross-legged in a tall closet, at my grandmother's house, where there were stacks and stacks of decorating magazines and scrapbooks, or as a teen sitting on my mother's poster bed with the current copy of *Vogue*. At the time I saw them as just beautiful rooms, but in returning to these images again and again, I realized how these spaces and the women living in them have shaped the way we look at rooms today. For Evangeline Bruce it was decorating with yards of silk ribbon, using their lengths to hang her beloved paintings. This seemingly discreet decorating choice not only was beautiful in effect but also served to weave a personal touch through the austere spaces of the ambassadorial residences in which she lived—in essence, putting her stamp on these rooms.

How They Decorated looks at sixteen women defined by four distinct decorating styles. Some of the women had the ability to inhabit several categories while others were strongly indicative of one particular style. *How They Decorated* explores these four categories: Legacy Style, In the Grand Manner, Fashionably Chic, and Unconventional Eye. Some of the rooms are well documented—having been photographed in different guises and over time—while other rooms, minimally documented and only glimpsed briefly, give us mere hints of their splendor.

Mona Williams von Bismarck, wearing Balenciaga in her Paris apartment at the famed Hôtel Lambert, was the embodiment of the woman decorating in the grand manner.

Expatriate aesthete Nancy Lancaster, an inspiration for the women of Legacy Style, declared her (decorating) independence while never straying far from her Virginia roots. Lancaster believed in an ideal of beauty, seeking it through the decoration of her houses by fusing elegance with comfort. Fashion designer Sybil Connolly cited Lancaster as her model when it came to decorating and drew from her own ancestral roots, using Irish antiques and comfortable chairs covered in chintz. Pieces from Evangeline Bruce's collection, like a portrait of Marie Antoinette, were seen over the decades in residences she lived in across the Continent with her husband. To create warmth in often austere rooms, Bruce, like Lancaster, employed tall flowering plants and trees in her formal and private spaces. She sought out decorator John Fowler, Lancaster's associate, to consult on subtle alterations to the American embassy in London when her husband was appointed ambassador there. A well-lived life was the credo of Legacy Style women, and the rooms they lived in were all given equal importance.

Like Louis XV's legendary mistress Madame de Pompadour, Mona von Bismarck decorated In the Grand Manner. As with all women decorating in this mode, the women represented here set the style rather than followed it, always keeping an eye to classic design. As if re-creating François Boucher's noted portrait of de Pompadour, photographer Cecil Beaton captured von Bismarck wearing Balenciaga in the grand rooms of her Hôtel Lambert apartment in Paris. An exuberant eighteenth-century Chinese paper dominated Baroness Pauline de Rothschild's *salon vert*, but beguiling subtleties were given equal importance by the baroness. Floors of parquet de Versailles were left bare except for a singular gold-shot tapestry. And, as with all things in *le style Pauline*, the tapestry was used idiosyncratically, placed on the floor as a carpet. Irises, de Rothschild's favorite flower, were arranged in Ming vases, which were placed on straw trays on the floor, extending the landscape of the wallpaper. Sensitivity to such minute details is a hallmark of decorating In the Grand Manner.

The great American decorator Billy Baldwin said of the ultra-chic Babe Paley, "She might have been painted by Boldini or by Picasso during his Rose Period." Wherever Paley was at any moment, she was sure to be surrounded by stylish rooms—the habitat of the Fashionably Chic. Baldwin created a tented fantasy for Paley and her husband at their New York pied-à-terre by shirring a printed cotton on the walls of the room. Later, Baldwin repeated this room at the Paley's Fifth Avenue home; indeed, this interior is one of his most noted to design aficionados. Fashion designer Elsa Schiaparelli collaborated with great interior designers of her day to decorate her Parisian residence, and, like all Fashionably Chic women's interiors, her rooms were filled with more than just a soupçon of fantasy, leaving no illusion as to her desire to make an indelible impression on her guests.

Photographer Horst P. Horst captured a distillation of Pauline de Rothschild's refined design
aesthetic—the pure and elegant combination, in the *salon vert* of her Paris apartment,
of a parquet de Versailles floor, faux-tortoise-shell baseboards, a tray with straw matting,
exquisite Chinese wall covering, and stems of bearded iris tinged with gold and brown.

The most divergent women in the collection are those with an Unconventional Eye. Dominique de Menil paired a Philip Johnson–designed house with an infusion of Charles James's high-fashion sensibility and the best of American Victorian furniture. Georgia O'Keeffe, great American artist and iconoclast, found an entirely new approach to her art in New Mexico. She witnessed the intrinsic complexities of the nature that surrounded her, all of which became part of her decoration. The placement and grouping of stones she collected in the desert were as meticulous and meaningful as the canvases that emerged from these and other objects found in the landscape.

The women of *How They Decorated* set out to make their rooms beautiful and in doing so they made an indelible mark on the way we look at our own rooms today. This book peers into almost a hundred rooms and explores countless variations of mode. There is a wide array of tastes represented—some of the rooms will speak to you while others perhaps not so much. But within each there is a raison d'être, and all exemplify deeply personal expressions of vision and beauty.

OPPOSITE: Evangeline Bruce brought classic American decoration to Winfield House in London's Regent's Park. ABOVE, LEFT: Babe Paley's own brand of glamour was evident in her rooms at her Billy Baldwin–designed apartment in New York's St. Regis hotel. ABOVE, RIGHT: Georgia O'Keeffe artfully displayed rocks from the desert at her house in New Mexico.

Legacy
STYLE

The women of Legacy Style owe much of their decorating prowess to past generations. Identifying with the faded grandeur of the ancestral home, these women embrace the objects they inherited as well as those evoking the period houses they lived in. The atmosphere of their rooms draws them to family heirlooms, both priceless and sentimental, or to faithful copies appearing in their rooms time and again. Preferring the old and ignoring au courant decorating modes—as did Nancy Lancaster, the great American-born doyenne of English-country decorating—these women delight in the lived-in intimacy of rooms that look untouched for generations. As Lancaster stated emphatically, "I can't bear anything that looks like it's been decorated." The ladies of Legacy Style would agree.

LADY DIANA COOPER

EVANGELINE BRUCE

LOUISE DE VILMORIN

SYBIL CONNOLLY

LADY DIANA COOPER

Sublime Englishness

DIANA OLIVIA WINIFRED MAUD MANNERS (1892–1986), BORN to the Marquess and Marchioness of Granby (later the 8th Duke and Duchess of Rutland), was reared to be a king's consort, but her storied life took her from her ancestral home, Belvoir Castle in Leicestershire, to her first home in Bloomsbury as a newlywed, then to many years abroad as a diplomat's wife and finally back to England. An early suitor called her "an orchid among cowslips, a black tulip in a garden of cucumbers, nightshade in the day nursery." An impressionable young Diana flowered in homes decorated by her ethereal artist mother, Violet, a member of the much-lauded late nineteenth-century set known as The Souls. Diana Manners, who would grow up to be the established beauty of the day with pools of blue for eyes, golden hair, and porcelain skin, kept the society pages buzzing. Later, Cecil Beaton wrote, "Lady Diana Cooper is one of the few living aristocrats who can violate all the rules and still keep her balance on the pedestal of noblesse oblige. Her roots are so deeply embedded in tradition that, like some incredible plant, she thrives in an atmosphere of bohemianism without ever departing from her origins."

Number 16 Arlington Street, early home to the Manners family, was a stately James Gibbs mansion with interiors by William Kent overlooking Green Park in London. The elegant place was turned on its ear by her mother's works of art decorating every room. When Lady Diana's father became the Duke of Rutland, the ancestral home of Belvoir was the backdrop for her adolescence and coming out. As a young girl Diana was allowed to decorate her room at the castle—the results were dramatic, with "a narrow four-poster bed for my new room at Belvoir, which was

Lady Diana, a true English rose, was considered the most beautiful woman of her time.
Cecil Beaton wrote, "She had this magic quality—chic isn't the word."

Lady Diana and her mother, Violet, the Duchess of Rutland, painted a Chinese-style mural on the walls of Diana's bathroom at the Coopers' London town house. The luxurious room was fitted out with a sofa, Regency chairs, and a lidded bathtub.

to be painted black. The bed was upholstered in red damask. . . . The black walls were hung with swags of everlasting flowers *à la* Crivelli. . . . There were coloured reproductions of Madonnas in gold Italian frames and the candlesticks from Florence. . . . I thought it was beyond compare, but greatly feared criticism."

Dramatic flourishes would always accompany her most sedate of decorating schemes, along with the pastels her mother had loved to dress her in, always playing up Diana's features to best effect. "My mother never damped our taste—she who had so influenced it."

Lady Diana married politician and diplomat Duff Cooper, one of the few men of her coterie who had survived the horrors of the First World War. Unheard of amongst her set, Diana, as a young wife, turned actress, playing the Madonna in a revival of *The Miracle*, touring in America and Germany in the 1920s. Her career earnings helped

decorate the Coopers' first residence on Gower Street, eventually expanding it several times. Her bedroom and "drawing-room-sized" bathroom were eked out of an adjacent flat, and later an additional flat was converted into a bedroom and sitting room for Duff. With her mother's artistry, the bathroom was decorated in the Chinese style. "We took a tracing of a Chinese paper at Belvoir and together on ladders we painted the white trees and birds and cages and butterflies on a pale green ground. It had a marble perspectived balustrade and, as at Belvoir, a marbled dado. The bath was hidden in a lidded coffer marbled to match. There was a large sofa, a pretty fireplace and gilded looking-glasses. . . . I felt a queen in a fairy story and could not ask for more."

After spending time in London at the beginning of the Second World War, Lady Diana retreated to the countryside near Bognor, where she had a cottage that she had

One of several chinoiserie wallpapers at Lady Diana's ancestral home, Belvoir Castle in Leicestershire, the King's Room paper was the inspiration for her bathroom walls (opposite) at the Gower Street residence she shared with her husband, Duff, in London.

OPPOSITE: The library at the Hôtel de Charost, the British ambassador's residence in Paris, as it appears today was much the same when the Coopers were in residence. Christian Bérard constructed the non-supporting columns out of hollow tubes—a postwar economy. The gilding and tortoise-shell finishes were inspired by a palace in Saint Petersburg.

ABOVE: Cecil Beaton photographed Lady Diana in repose on Pauline Borghese's Empire bed at the ambassadorial residence, while her husband served as ambassador after the Second World War.

inherited from her mother. She described it as a "Regency bungalow," and added two large rooms "lighted by Gothic-topped windows in character with the house." Cecil Beaton's bucolic photographs of Lady Diana during the period with her doing her bit for the cause were real enough. Never one to languish, she procured a cow, chickens, beehives, and goats and started farming. As the war slogged on, husband Duff Cooper's career at the British foreign office exported her to Singapore and Algiers, where her bedroom became "the club," with Randolph Churchill

and Evelyn Waugh often joining her for breakfast on her bed. The pinnacle of Duff Cooper's career was serving as British ambassador in postwar France as a French provisional government was established. The Hôtel de Charost, on the rue du Faubourg Saint-Honoré, would be home to the Coopers for four years. Lady Diana slept in Pauline Borghese's grand Empire bed, saying, "As I get older, I get more susceptible to beauty of surroundings." Recalling the ox-blood Borghese decorations, she wrote, "Walls, curtains, sofas and chairs were upholstered in the richest Lyons silk which bore a design of caducei and laurel-leaves." As ambassadress,

ABOVE and OPPOSITE: Trompe-l'oeil panels, painted in acrylic on aluminum by Martin Battersby, dominated the walls of Lady Diana's Little Venice, London, dining room. The intricate paintings, which had been created for a previous residence, featured motifs that referenced the couple's history together, with grisaille Baroque-inspired trophies and colorfully detailed objects painted over the armorials. The carved settee began life in the drawing room of the Coopers' Gower Street residence

Lady Diana loved the social whirl and entertained as lavishly as postwar Paris would allow. The creation of Duff Cooper's embassy library in 1946–47 by Charles de Beistegui, in collaboration with Georges Geffroy and Christian Bérard, was a triumph.

From the ambassador's residence, the Coopers moved to Château de Saint-Firmin in Chantilly, where Lady Diana decorated the grand rooms of the eighteenth-century manor house in her pleasing style, with pieces accumulated from her past residences and some from the embassy. With the elegance of an embassy, coupled with the relaxed feel of the English countryside, the house welcomed the Coopers' many friends. Lady Diana had painter Martin Battersby create a series of enchanting trompe-l'oeil panels, which featured objects relating to the Coopers' history together. She brought these panels with her when she returned to London in 1960.

"I came home after about ten years, alas! alone, and found myself a house I would exchange with no other in the best of all quarters—Little Venice." The house was quite small compared to the houses Lady Diana previously had inhabited—but full of charm. The Battersby panels covered the walls in the dining room. With plenty of family portraits, like Sir James Jebusa Shannon's portraits of the Duchess of Rutland as a priestess and young Diana in black velvet and a vandyke collar, the living room echoed the elegance of its resident to perfection. A little bar was set up in the hall just outside the living room, with a portrait of Lady Diana by Ambrose McEvoy hanging over it; the walls were finished in a loose stylized trompe-l'oeil marble with proper moldings.

Documented so uniquely in the Martin Battersby panels, Lady Diana's equally uncommon life was filled with a multitude of houses, friends, and memories. She tells all in a seven-hundred-page autobiography. But Lady Diana could elegantly describe life in a single phrase: "First you are young; then you are middle-aged; then you are old; then you are wonderful."

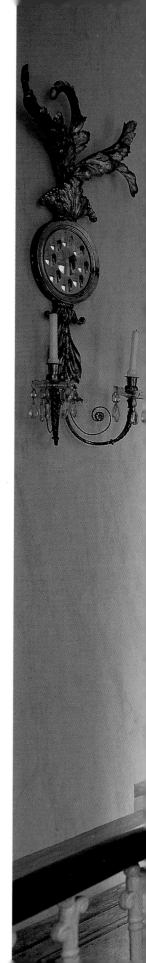

RIGHT: Trompe-l'oeil marble walls, moldings, and baseboards in the hall off the living room of the house in Little Venice, London, transformed the small space. Ignoring formal design conventions (although wonderfully convenient), a bar was placed on the wall. Ambrose McEvoy's romantic portrait of Lady Diana hung over the bar.

FOLLOWING SPREAD: The snug Little Venice living room was partially separated from the dining area with a well-worn screen. Markedly English, the furniture in front of the fireplace was covered in different chintzes.

LEFT: Lady Diana wrote, "I like [bedrooms] best . . . with a big bed and tiny dog—still, and as always, a refuge. It is the room I'm the most attached—offering repose, sleep, privacy, or receiving of friends." Her personal emblem, the unicorn, was emblazoned on the wastebasket and painted on a lampshade.

ABOVE: Lady Diana stacked her fashion accessory of choice—hats—on a chest of drawers in her London bedroom. One topped a bust of a young Diana, which had been sculpted by her mother.

EVANGELINE BRUCE

American Classic

EVANGELINE BRUCE (1914–1995), CALLED "THE TRUE QUEEN OF American style" by publisher and editor John Fairchild, ruled with understated elegance, an aura of mystery, and an erudite personality—which were perfectly reflected in the rooms she created across the world for three decades. Her husband, David K. E. Bruce, an American diplomat and ambassador to Britain, France, Germany, and China, found in Evangeline his perfect companion. Greatly admired and famous for her Washington parties, she was her husband's equal in diplomatic finesse, but her private world revolved more steadily around longstanding friendships and the expansive environments she created.

Born to her role, Evangeline could have effectively posed for eighteenth-century painter Thomas Gainsborough. Jacqueline Kennedy Onassis described her as having the "grace and imagination and the virtues of another time." As a child, she lived in countless countries; her lessons were in French and walks with her nanny were along the Great Wall of China. Having studied at Radcliffe, her fluency in multiple languages placed her in the Office of Strategic Services in London during the Second World War, where she created backgrounds for forged documents used by English spies in France. An English friend described Evangeline as "the most European and yet the most American woman I have ever met. There is nothing expatriate about her. Her American roots balance her, give [her life] its simplicity and disregard for the sumptuous." Her sense of style and attention to detail easily translated into her personal decorating lexicon.

Akin to the relaxed atmosphere of an English country house, Evangeline's homes took on very personal statements—difficult in ambassadorial residences

Standing by a portrait of Thomas Jefferson at Winfield House in London's Regent's Park, Evangeline Bruce posed with her dogs for photographer Cecil Beaton.

where furniture was often provided and art was on loan. While rooms could have easily slipped into anonymity, all of the Bruce homes carried the mark of Evangeline and her husband's strong, eclectic design aesthetic. She collected Oriental and European antiques—acquisitions becoming "close friends" and portable possessions, as a peripatetic diplomat's wife, reflecting her individuality. Ribbons accompanied paintings and tall potted plants filled rooms that were deceptively uncalculated, yet Mrs. Bruce's deft hand was ever present in the creation of each subtle juxtaposition. Flowering plants—primarily fuchsias, camellias, and heliotropes, all seasonally appropriate—were integral to the decoration.

Perhaps the Bruces' most prestigious appointment was to the Court of Saint James in 1961. Certainly Winfield House, the United States ambassador's residence in London's Regent's Park, was the most imposing diplomatic residence they occupied. Built in 1936, the formal rooms were filled with Adam-style decorations, elements of classical architecture, and French boiseries. With the Bruces' personal collections, Winfield's stately rooms were given over to warmth. John Fowler—who was to become a friend of Evangeline and David—was called in to make the mansion their own.

Their Albany residence, with interiors by Fowler, was home to the couple after leaving Winfield House in 1969. Taking cues from his client's refined sensibilities and her knowledge of the French Revolution and Napoleon's reign, Fowler based the set of rooms on a Louis XVI apartment. He chose an Italianate yellow for the drawing room walls and created elaborate curtains made of silk faille in oyster and draw curtains in apricot silk, influenced by an eighteenth-century wedding dress.

The Bruces' family home when in Washington, DC, was an early nineteenth-century Federal house in Georgetown, with eleven thousand square feet. Through the years, Evangeline called on Fowler to help with certain details in the house. Curtains with pinked edges, which Fowler had designed for their Brussels residence, were reused in a hallway. Once a thirty-four-foot-long ballroom, the Georgetown drawing room, which opened onto Mrs. Bruce's beautiful gardens, was filled with a connoisseur's collection of beloved objects from around the world. Lavish yet subdued patterns and repeated tones of chartreuse, cantaloupe, and brown enriched the mix of Continental antiques. Special paintings and furniture reappeared in the Georgetown house after having served in other residences, particularly a pair of eighteenth-century leather screens and a pair of Gothick chairs that had once belonged to Nancy Lancaster. Evangeline Bruce relied heavily on sumptuous skirted tables in rich colors to soften formal rooms.

Friend Jacqueline Kennedy Onassis wrote in a note to Mrs. Bruce, "One was so proud as an

Evangeline Bruce's drawing room at Albany, a mansion of private residences in London, as decorated by John Fowler in shades of yellow and blue. A gift from her decorator, two fiberglass jars with her initials emblazoned on them were placed atop a pair of delicate brackets. Her signature ribbons decorated an eighteenth-century portrait of an Englishman in Indian dress on the Grand Tour.

ABOVE and RIGHT: On a table in the Bruces' Albany drawing room photographs of their life in the diplomatic world were displayed alongside an 'Evangeline Bruce' rose and a small architectural drawing in a gilt frame. A Dutch screen in somber tones served as a counterpoint to the more vibrant colors of the room. From their many years of service abroad, the Bruces had thoughtfully collected paintings and antiques on the Continent and in England, some exhibiting the patina of time and general use. Evangeline Bruce loved each and every piece, commenting, "I don't mind mended things."

American to think that other countries recognized you as our very best." With such accolades (and a permanent place in the International Best-Dressed Hall of Fame), Evangeline Bruce wasn't about to fade into a life of retirement; in the final year of her life, she published a book twenty years in the making, *Napoleon and Josephine: An Improbable Marriage*. In spite of her peregrine life, and maybe because of the commitment she had to her own marriage, Evangeline created surroundings that were full of treasured objects, order, and beauty.

LEFT and ABOVE: A corner of the drawing room at the Bruces' Albany apartment, called a set, looking into the dining room. Ribbons paired with paintings created a whimsical sophistication, an example of the elegance that Evangeline Bruce was famous for. The intimate dining room featured a central table piled with books, when not in use for meals, and special pieces from the Bruce collection: a portrait of Marie Antoinette over the mantel and a portrait of Selim III of Turkey.

OPPOSITE: The Albany library, decorated by Diana Phipps, was used extensively by Evangeline Bruce. A printed fabric in the exotic shades of the East was used on the walls and cupboards, taking inspiration from a copy of a seventeenth-century painting of Pocahontas in Jacobean dress.

ABOVE: The cantaloupe-colored walls of the Georgetown (Washington, DC) drawing room were a backdrop for Bruce antiques. The Gothick chairs once belonged to decorating doyenne Nancy Lancaster, and in a nod to Lancaster, Bruce used ribbons to decorate and unify the paintings.

Cecil Beaton described
Evangeline Bruce's style
in decorating and clothes
as "unfussy, deliciously
coloured, and internationally
eclectic." These tenets
dominated the Georgetown
drawing room. According
to Bruce, the colors of the
room's decoration were "the
outside of a cantaloupe,
and the walls a cantaloupe's
inside." Curtains designed
by John Fowler for the
Albany apartment were
integrated into the room
with aplomb.

LOUISE DE VILMORIN

Timeless Seduction

LOUISE LÉVÊQUE DE VILMORIN (1902–1969) WAS AN HEIRESS, author, paramour to the famous, and noted chatelaine of Château de Vilmorin in Verrières-le-Buisson, France. The château, known as Verrières, had been built as a hunting lodge for Louis XIV in 1680, but served ostensibly as a rendezvous for the king and his young mistress Louise de la Vallière. Later it was surrounded by botanical gardens installed by the Vilmorin family after they purchased it in 1815. Though Louise de Vilmorin lived many places around the world, the family château of Verrières, both labyrinthine—composed of salons, libraries, attics, and lofts—and unchanging, remained her *domaine suprême*. Ever the romantic poet, Vilmorin said, "Every room is haunted with souvenirs that mean so much."

The Salon Bleu, the main salon of the house, was deliciously smothered in a French floral print by Georges Le Manach, called simply Batik and based on the indigo resist-printed textiles of India that had been introduced into Europe during the seventeenth century. Vilmorin planned the room with designer Henri Samuel in the early 1950s. In 1965, Ninette Lyon, writing for American *Vogue*, attributed the cornflower blue of the print as Louise de Vilmorin's "Verrières Blue." The rambling floral chintz in blue and white, has since become forever bound to Louise de Vilmorin for design aesthetes. Acknowledging the timeless design scheme, Vilmorin stocked sufficient yardage of the fabric at the château for future generations to reupholster the room's furniture and remake its curtains.

The furniture in Vilmorin's Salon Bleu ranged from Louis Seize to Second Empire. Placed in front of the room's fireplace was a Second Empire *fauteuil indiscret*, perfect for

Louise de Vilmorin, wearing a flowing caftan and an exotic choker, posed for Cecil Beaton in the Verrières dining room surrounded by family heirlooms.

a Vilmorin tête-à-tête. The upholstered chairs were elaborately fringed and tasseled, and the scalloped border of the fabric was used in artful ways. Everything was done up in the striking print—nothing was spared her own brand of Vilmorin ancestral chic.

Vilmorin knew everyone who was anyone. She captivated many of those whom she met but was also described by Evelyn Waugh as "an Hungarian countess who pretended to be a French poet. An egocentric maniac with the eyes of a witch"—these being the kinds of inevitable darts thrown at women whose lives are lived in opposition to polite society. The lady described her passion—writing—in terms of her sexual conquests, saying that each conquest "lights my lantern, that's what pushed me to write." Vilmorin drew great men to her "lantern," namely Antoine de Saint-Exupéry, author of *Le Petit Prince*; American actor Orson Welles; British ambassador Duff Cooper; and André Malraux, novelist and later minister for cultural affairs in France. Lady Diana Cooper, Duff's wife, nevertheless devoted a bedroom at the residence exclusively for Vilmorin's use, saying, "This forty-year-old genius . . . loves us both with so much passion, tenderness, monomania, that her friends think she's mad."

LEFT: Christian Bérard, French artist and friend to Vilmorin, illustrated her "decorating with heirlooms" style. Vilmorin often accompanied her signature with a trademark clover.

OPPOSITE: The femme fatale Louise de Vilmorin lounged on an ottoman in her Salon Bleu holding her talisman clover. Vilmorin often dressed in piquantly girlish dress: ribbons, cardigans, ruffled collars, and dirndl skirts. The Verrières salon with its romantic Le Manach print was as decorative and enchanting as its chatelaine.

Louise de Vilmorin did take time out from her passionate affairs for poetic decorating. Adopting the four-leaf clover as a personal trademark, Vilmorin had it appliquéd onto masses of white damask napkins by D. Porthault, used during her legendary Sunday night suppers. The venerated French company, inspired by the commission, introduced the Les Trèfles pattern to its line. Her china was also emblazoned with the lucky talisman.

Vilmorin had the interior walls of the château washed with the colors of eggshell: browns, blues, and greens. She then filled niches and alcoves with family oddities that attracted her—each object being given significant attention. In the dining room, lavishly decorated in the Gothic style of Charles X, massive chairs stood along the walls, their backs shaped like towering Gothic arches carved with roundels. A collection of fish in silver, some measuring over a yard, hung on the walls along with silver chargers and sconces. Silver beakers and goblets filled the room in cabinets and on tables. A menagerie of animals in silver mounted on malachite plinths and Bavarian silver, hallmarked Augsburg, marched down the dining table.

Most of what Louise de Vilmorin did was approved of by the men who frequented Verrières, certainly her three adoring brothers who returned to the family château often. Another enchanted visitor was Murray Douglas, a member of the Brunschwig family. She recalls being taken by her aunt, Zelina Brunschwig, to the Salon Bleu at Verrières to meet Vilmorin, her aunt admonishing her niece, "Don't talk, just look." The pair would instate the fabric Verrières into the Brunschwig & Fils fabric line and Murray would decorate her own rooms in the print.

Inspired by Verrières, other women of note, including Hélène Rochas and Nadine de Rothschild, chose the iconic chintz. Rothschild described the print as "a country pattern, very feminine. I couldn't use it in the city or with a man around the house. I must admit that in buying [my cottage in Brittany] I was thinking of the fabric. When I first saw it at Louise de Vilmorin's, it seemed to go perfectly with her, and then I discovered that Hélène Rochas had the same fabric, too. That made me realize that it made all the women look lovelier because it radiates a peaceful and serene atmosphere."

I doubt if Louise de Vilmorin would have agreed with that assessment of its atmosphere; in fact, she would have objected vehemently, meting out her judgment with a poison pen. With absolute confidence in her botanist brothers and their never raising any objection whatsoever to flowers, Vilmorin filled the now legendary room with the bounty of the floral print. The result was eternal and effortless—as was Vilmorin herself.

OPPOSITE: The repetition of the rambling floral print in the now legendary Salon Bleu unified disparate furniture styles and the family's eclectic collections. Furniture maker Lucien Alavoine made the black lacquered table, with blue-and-white porcelain insets, to Vilmorin's specifications.

FOLLOWING SPREAD: Indicative of the Vilmorin paradigm, styles in the Salon Bleu ranged from Empire to the late nineteenth century. Vilmorin said, "We still love and revere our grandmother and could never treat her house in a way she would not have liked."

ABOVE: Variations of the Vilmorin dining room were photographed and interpreted in illustrations over the years. The Vilmorin family reveled in serving their guests at table and were famous for their Sunday night suppers.

OPPOSITE: A massive Empire table with a circular green marble top held the family's silver gilt menagerie: a swan, owls, and monkeys made by eighteenth-century silversmith Odiot that were both decorative and functional as receptacles for holding flowers, sugar, and salt.

SYBIL CONNOLLY

Irish Elegance

SYBIL CONNOLLY (1921–1998) CALLED HER DUBLIN HOUSE and fashion atelier at 71 Merrion Square "the house that linen built." In truth, it was Connolly's talent for channeling the native crafts of Ireland during the 1950s that built her a fashion empire, the first of its kind in Ireland.

Sybil moved with her mother from Wales to Ireland at the age of fifteen, and to London at seventeen to apprentice with a dressmaker. She began her ascent into the world of haute couture when she returned to Ireland with the outbreak of the Second World War. Connolly, her own best model, had the uncanny ability to present herself—and her designs—steeped in mythic romanticism. Her first major fashion show, in 1953, was held at Dunsany Castle, County Meath, the home of her client Sheila, Lady Dunsany. Handwoven woolens made in cottages across Ireland and gossamer lace made by Carrickmacross nuns enhanced her effortless designs. Connolly deftly used traditional Irish textiles and reinterpreted them. Tweed would be whitewashed. Clones lace was used as an embellishment on linen evening blouses. Connolly transformed brilliant scarlet flannel, inspired by the petticoats of women from Connemara, into voluminous capes and skirts. The unique Connolly mix of cambric, satin, and Irish poplin for blouses and ball skirts was just the thing stylish Irish aristocrats could embrace for their round of fancy parties, and this sophisticated mix especially appealed to fashionable Americans. During Connolly's reign as Ireland's self-appointed ambassador to the world of fashion, Ireland's prime minister called her "Ireland's national treasure." Dignitaries and celebrities from all over the world made pilgrimages to Merrion Square when in Ireland.

Legendary Irish fashion designer Sybil Connolly believed one should "use nothing that startles; beauty is the only stimulation needed."

Sybil Connolly's decorating style was as traditional and appropriate as the clothes she designed—"I feel, really, that if I had my time over again I might have done interior decorating rather than fashion designing," she once said. She filled her Georgian mansion on Merrion Square with Adam-style moldings and plasterwork. Her 1954 collection included skirts that mimicked the ornate plasterwork ceiling designs of the house. The first-floor drawing room was given over to her professional life—a boutique where clients called and fashion shows were held. Tissue-thin pale gray Irish linen tinged with lilac was applied to the walls, echoing the pleated linen she made famous with her dress designs. With nine yards of the finest handkerchief linen pleated into one single yard, it took thousands of yards to cover the walls, making for an unforgettably romantic backdrop to her equally romantic clothes. Connolly called it a "sensation." Honoring her husband's Irish roots, First Lady Jacqueline Kennedy chose one of Connolly's pleated linen designs to wear for her official White House portrait by Aaron Shikler.

Above the atelier's two floors, two additional floors were Connolly's private rooms. In period style, her living room was serenely eighteenth century, echoing her sentiment that "the eighteenth-century feeling is the mood I happen to enjoy most. That century was such a prolific period for good design." Reflecting Irish charm in her rooms was of the utmost importance to her, and she never compromised. Sybil Connolly lived in all her rooms, regardless of formality. She hated pretentious houses, saying, "I can't bear that feeling. . . . The ideal house should look lived in, as if somebody reads the books on the shelves." She cited Nancy Lancaster's rooms as being her most admired, writing, "She has the almost incomparable facility of putting together a room and creating a casual perfection. The fabric and furniture invariably look so right—as though they had come home—that they create a pleasing and attractive power." Taking decorating cues from Lancaster and tapping into her refined gifts as a hostess, Connolly captivated guests with her enchanting surroundings and faultless charm.

Her house was filled with collections guided by the rich history of Irish decorative arts. In collecting Irish delftware—considered rare, as it was only made in and around Dublin for less than two decades in the mid-eighteenth century—she considered herself to be something of an expert. Connolly's delftware reflected her pleasure in collecting rare pieces: "I love it. It's fun collecting something you can't get." (Although she usually got what she wanted.) Connolly disdained anything modern, dismissing the Warhols of the era. She, however, did feel the best of any period could insert itself effortlessly into a room. Having

A portrait of Sybil Connolly by Simon Elwes graced a hall in her Merrion Square town house in Dublin. The walls were papered in a trompe-l'oeil draped fabric that dramatically contrasted with the whitewashed Adam-style plasterwork. Chinese export porcelain and shells as decoration appeared throughout Connolly's rooms.

In the drawing room Connolly covered the walls in a pleated Irish linen in the same mode of her signature pleated-linen ball skirts and dresses. She reminisced about the decoration of the house writing, "So when I came to doing the house, I thought to myself, perhaps I should do the house with this feeling in mind—to dig deep into what we've got in Ireland and see what I can use in interior decorating."

created her own collections of china and other decorative pieces in the 1970s, she didn't mind beautiful reproductions. Old Irish silver was another passion, with one fine piece of Sicilian silver from about AD 700 interjecting itself into her collection. Connolly's 1994 book *Irish Hands: The Tradition of Beautiful Crafts* traced the origins of these crafts and featured them in the rooms of Merrion Square and its neighboring mews house.

The mews house, with its adjoining gardens leading to the main house at Merrion Square, appeared as if it had been there forever, but Connolly had planned it with the assistance of two craftsmen. A living room ran the entire width of the eighteenth-century-style structure. There Connolly used warmer colors she referred to as "fresh

and cheerful and easy to live with." Color played an influential part in her rooms and her fashion designs. Connolly evoked an idyllic Ireland, with lyrical names for her designs: Dark Lake, Jane Eyre, Moss Green, Autumn Violet, Deerstalker, Tattersal, Black Tulip, Turncoat, Gillymot, Brown Peach, Flax Flower, Apple Snow, Gorse, and Irish Moss.

When fashion began to change in the early 1960s, Sybil Connolly reinvented herself, parlaying her Irish charm into collections of porcelain, crystal, wallpapers and fabrics, and other decorative objects for the home. Her china pattern for Tiffany & Company, called Merrion Square, featured a black border with botanicals, styled after an embroidered court dress belonging to Mary Delany, an eighteenth-century English

On the top floor of her Dublin town house an ambience of lived-in coziness pervaded, and the low ceilings contributed to the intimacy and warmth. Though she decorated the rooms of her town house and the adjoining mews house herself, she adored the design work of John Fowler and Nancy Lancaster. In characteristic Lancaster style, Sybil Connolly decorated with soft chintzes, porcelains, and fine antiques.

aristocrat and artist. She designed wallpapers and fabrics for Brunschwig & Fils and, later, bed linens for Martex. Her collections for Brunschwig & Fils were inspired by the interior restoration work she did for the cottage orné of the 1st Earl of Glengall, who had built it around 1810 after a design by Regency architect John Nash. Along with producing her extensive decorative collections, Connolly wrote and edited books and articles about Irish houses, gardens, and decoration, continuing to advocate the beauty of Irish craftsmanship. Like Evelyn Gleeson, a prominent figure in the Celtic arts and crafts revival in 1895, Connolly had "come back to Ireland to find work for Irish hands in the making of beautiful things." With real conviction, Sybil Connolly felt decoration should be "dictated by the house to a certain extent—and happily so." What more could be expected of a national treasure?

OPPOSITE and ABOVE: Connolly's dining room was furnished with all things Irish, from the eighteenth and early nineteenth centuries. A wallpaper adorned with fuchsias covered the walls, Connolly having fallen in love with the flower that grows wild in the Irish countryside. China from her collection for Tiffany & Company graced the table alongside Irish crystal, linens, and silver. She wrote that she had to close her eyes when she had the antique mahogany table ebonized to match the period Regency chairs.

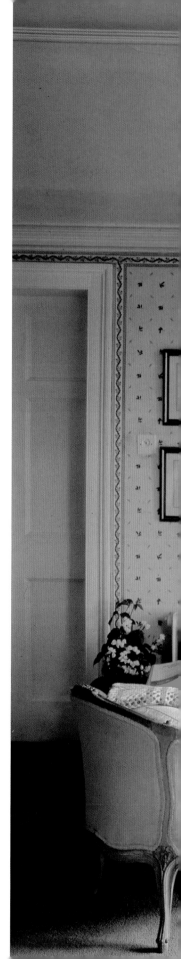

ABOVE and OPPOSITE: Sybil Connolly used shells, alongside Chinese export porcelain, as decoration in her bedroom. The patterned wallpaper was inspired by her collection of French "Angoulême" porcelain. She had the pattern printed on linen and made in Ireland. Nancy Lancaster so loved the room that she wrote, "May I copy your bedroom?" Connolly had to have been thrilled, considering Lancaster was her ideal when it came to decorating. A chaise longue—covered in her favorite color, green—was piled with embroidered Irish linen pillows.

FOLLOWING SPREAD: The living room walls of Connolly's mews house were painted an apricot yellow. Shell-adorned moldings reflected her love of the motif as a decorative device. The room's floor was sectioned off into hexagons and painted to resemble marble. Her Mildred chintz, with camellias and honeysuckles, designed for Robert Allen, covered seating and pillows. Connolly also designed the eighteenth-century-style faux-painted mantel for the room.

In the Grand
MANNER

No other collection of women is quite as stringent in its approach to design as the women decorating In the Grand Manner. Touted by fashion editors as the women most likely to be on the best-dressed lists, they live in the most desired houses in the most desirable locations. These women are devoted to their fashion designers, as well as their own design aesthetics. Marrying money or born with it, they believe in luxury, drama, and the sweeping grand statement. Slaves to perfection, these women can obsess over every detail. Most of Pauline de Rothschild's rooms were personal sanctuaries, yet they were always camera ready. The ladies living In the Grand Manner exemplify Elsie de Wolfe's statement: "A woman's environment will speak for her life, whether she likes it or not."

HÉLÈNE ROCHAS

GABRIELLE VAN ZUYLEN

MONA VON BISMARCK

PAULINE DE ROTHSCHILD

HÉLÈNE ROCHAS

Cosmopolitan Chic

HÉLÈNE ROCHAS (1927–2011), WIFE OF COUTURIER MARCEL Rochas, was sublimely characterized by French Surrealist poet Paul Éluard as *presque fée* (almost a fairy). Only eighteen when she married, she developed her design taste after her husband's refined sense of style. It was Marcel Rochas—along with decorator Georges Geffroy—who set their rue Barbet-de-Jouy *hôtel particulier* in Paris's 7th arrondissement on its elegant trajectory. Their daughter, Sophie, said of her father, "He was an artist to his fingertips, which meant he decided what my mother wore, the tablecloths, the menus, the porcelain." After Marcel Rochas's death in 1955, Hélène Rochas continued to refine her taste and decorating style, veering away from the Parisian chic characterized by *le grand goût français* with her own brand of cosmopolitanism. Hubert de Givenchy remembered Rochas's aesthetic, saying, "A new style was created, and it was truly a revelation. I would even say it was a revolution in taste." Hélène Rochas took the reins of the Rochas company when her husband died, establishing the Rochas perfume empire.

Hélène Rochas approached decoration as she approached her classic good looks, insisting on refinement but always staying on trend. Her impeccable art collection was set off with white walls and elegant period furniture. François de Ricqlès of Christie's in Paris described her taste as one "that has practically died out, in which styles and eras are brought together with elegance and sobriety. . . . I think it's extremely Parisian." The early apartment, influenced by her husband, was strictly Empire. A pair of Empire gueridons, once belonging to the noble family of Murat, stayed with Rochas for the more than six decades she lived at the residence, moving

Hélène Rochas, in an evening gown designed by her husband, Marcel Rochas, 1950. Over the decades her wardrobe would change with the times, but her refinement was constant.

only as far as a room. Here the foundation of her decorating aesthetic was created, an elegant juxtaposition of modern art with antiques. Rochas elaborated, "In Paris, in the years just after the Liberation, there was an explosion of exceptional talent. As luck would have it, I was surrounded by writers and painters. We were 'at home' every Monday in our first apartment, and the people invited to my salon made a brilliant and lifelong impression on me."

In the Paris apartment's petit salon, Balthus's painting *Japonaise à la table rouge* reflected the Rochas atmosphere of passion. In the 1970s the masterpiece hung in the study of her New York pied-à-terre against a backdrop of Braquenié's classic eighteenth-century pattern Le Rocher. A long low-slung sofa was covered in the same pattern. Floor-to-ceiling panels covered in the same bark pattern were ingeniously installed to glide across windows making for the illusion of a garden. "Here, green is my way of bringing nature inside," said Rochas. With the help of friend and interior designer François Catroux, she chose strong but spare pieces to evoke an air of serenity—synonymous with its owner. Art deco tables found harmony amid honeyed beige, olive, and her favored white—the color of the fabric the pair chose for the walls of the apartment.

An impeccable use of contrasting elements was also present in Paris. In her music room art deco pieces by Émile-Jacques Ruhlmann and Eileen Gray were set off by midnight-blue lacquered walls. Rochas, like Yves Saint Laurent and Pierre Bergé, had assembled a large collection of art deco works by the end of the 1960s. A more recent manifestation of the music room held few echoes of the previous one. The newly decorated room was a vision in white, filled with pieces by Diego Giacometti that she had used in the New York apartment in the 1970s.

Catroux summed up the brilliance of her particular style: "I was always surprised by the strictness of her taste for the stylish objects which surrounded her; it was almost masculine in its rigor: bare, strict, quite the opposite of what one could have expected from the femininity of her legendary beauty." For Hélène Rochas it was simply a matter of her endless pursuit for beauty: "I can't stop dreaming of making things more beautiful, more elegant—I can't resist changing a pumpkin into a coach."

Hélène Rochas's boudoir as it appeared in 1950 was decorated by Georges Geffroy with canvases painted after designs by the esteemed French wallpaper manufacturer Zuber. The scenes reflected the Empire scheme of the rue Barbet-de-Jouy residence. The lit à la polonaise, formally draped in satin, and eighteenth-century Georges Jacob–made cabriolet chairs adorned the formal room. A psyche, a tilted mirror named for the Greek goddess of the soul, in mahogany with brass candle holders, echoed the Empire themes.

PRECEDING SPREAD: Both sumptuous and spare, the living room of Rochas's New York apartment at the Olympic Tower looked out over the city. Interior designer François Catroux worked with Rochas to create rooms that reflected her renowned finesse. Rochas combined trends of the period with her world-class collections. A Diego Giacometti coffee table was paired with Italian chairs in the style of Louis XV alongside a comfortable chaise. Sliding screens covered in a tree of life–patterned fabric could be closed, covering the windows of the apartment.

LEFT: Creating a serene space, Catroux carved out a stunning study from an apartment bedroom and decorated the space using simple Chinese chairs and an art deco desk as a foil to the dynamic bark-pattern fabric on the walls and sofa. The Balthus painting had been shown just two years earlier in a New York gallery to sensational press.

ABOVE: Dressed to match, Hélène Rochas was as stunning in blue as the midnight blue walls of the music room in her Paris residence. Art deco luminaries Eileen Gray and Émile-Jacques Ruhlmann were represented in the chic room, and a Jean Fautrier painting hung over the sleek fireplace.

OPPOSITE: A trompe-l'oeil panel by Alexandre Serebriakoff hung over the mantel in the Paris dining room. Louis XV chairs copied from the collection of the consummate twentieth-century collector Carlos de Beistegui were painted white and upholstered in a verdant green leather. Rochas preferred intimate dinner parties and used a round mahogany table where a single candle was often the only centerpiece.

In contrast to her New York living
room, the grand salon of the Rochas
Paris house was decorated with
period Empire chairs covered in
warm shades of caramel and brown.
The addition of art deco pieces like
the René Crevel rug and snake lamps
by Edgar Brandt exhibited Hélène
Rochas's finesse in fusing styles.

In the 1960s, Hélène Rochas engaged Jean-Pierre Basile to oversee the decoration of her Paris offices. She stylistically matched the room—and the times—by wearing a modish color-blocked André Courrèges dress with a schoolgirl collar. Rochas was passionate about cutting-edge style; more than making it plausible, she made it credible.

Gabrielle van Zuylen

Sumptuous Modernity

THE GLAMOROUS GABRIELLE ANDRÉE IGLESIAS VALAYAS VAN Zuylen (1933–2010) lived in a rarified world of haute luxe. The Virginia-reared, Radcliffe-educated Gabrielle, muse to both Hubert de Givenchy and Yves Saint Laurent, was perfect at balancing American roots and a Dutch aristocratic title. Her husband, Baron Thierry, was brother to Marie-Hélène de Rothschild, a name synonymous with le goût Rothschild. Yet the van Zuylens' au courant style was in extreme contrast to Marie-Hélène's luxurious opulence. Rebels perhaps, the international couple veered away from the expected, setting themselves apart by choosing to live in streamlined, modern rooms.

Gabrielle van Zuylen preferred classic design—Halston was a favorite—yet never discounted the power of fantasy dressing, not hesitating to wear a Zandra Rhodes creation, saying "I found my style when I stopped listening to other people." Likewise, after seeing an apartment in New York by French interior designer François Catroux, she knew she had found the perfect collaborator to achieve the kind of modern rooms she loved and wanted to live in. Beyond the Paris apartment she shared with her husband and children, there was a modern house built on a working stud farm, Varaville, in Normandy, with the same spirit and understated panache.

With Catroux, the van Zuylens transformed dark nineteenth-century Paris rooms into sleek refined spaces of nonchalant chic. In an interview with *Vogue* in 1975, Gabrielle van Zuylen lauded the designer for the successful transformation of rooms that hadn't reflected their modern lifestyle. "It took someone like Catroux with an eye to rearrange all the volumes. All 300 square meters of the reception part had to be

---

Dressed in Emanuel Ungaro, Gabrielle van Zuylen posed for photographer David Massey in 1975 in her modernist Paris salon decorated by François Catroux.

blasted out—and he had the courage to do it." The resulting sweeping rooms—a long gallery, a salon, and an entrance—opened one onto another. "Cozy for two people, magnificent for thirty," said van Zuylen. "Now it all moves beautifully." The works of art in the apartment were of Gabrielle van Zuylen's own choosing, with Catroux designing around the collection. Clutter was expressly forbidden in a Catroux room, making it the perfect style to display her French Surrealist paintings. Alternating simple lines and textures with sensuous suedes and sleek surfaces, the French designer loathed the "decorator look," also an anathema to the van Zuylens.

The Normandy house, in indigenous stone and designed by French-based American architect Peter Harnden, was in stark contrast to the countryside's old-guard design aesthetic. It was a house that was at once livable and alive—practical yet luxurious. Wings of the house featured grass-sown rooftops that could be seen from Gabrielle's all-white bathroom. At Varaville, nature reigned inside and out. With expansive views of the estate through enormous panes of glass, the living room had stark white walls juxtaposed with natural stone. The walls were bare with the exception of a Roberto Matta abstract painting in the dining space. Slate floors and a sleek, dark teak ceiling defined the long room—no-nonsense and stylish at the same time. A Mies van der Rohe leather sofa in the living room, a library turned out in leather, and a leather handrail on a spiral staircase were consistent with the equine tack of a stud farm. Varaville could house the family—there were four daughters—and a number of guests with an easy elegance. "Nothing was missing. Even the choice of the books that were placed in their rooms was geared to the interest of the guest. Mom left nothing to chance," remembers one of her daughters. Relying on luxe surfaces, reflecting light, and a sense of timelessness, the house combined a classic resonance with modern energy.

Surrounding the low-slung copper-roofed house was a glorious garden designed by Russell Page. Van Zuylen became an expert in gardening from self-study and her friendship with Page. She authored the book *The Gardens of Russell Page*, where she documented the process of developing a garden, much like the process of building a house. In preparation for their collaboration on the Varaville garden, Page led her through museums, nurseries, and historic gardens, strengthening her passion and knowledge. The resulting gardens, five acres devoted to Page's vision, were as vibrant as the interiors, with Page achieving something just as unique to the countryside as the house and its interior. The importance that Gabrielle

Less is more—an obvious van Zuylen design rule and one employed in the baroness's bedroom in Normandy. Decorated in all white, it was a striking contrast to the green Russell Page–designed landscape visible beyond. Van Zuylen saw nature as a decorative element that would work in harmony with the room—not surprising since gardening was her passion. The design aesthetic of her friend Pauline de Rothschild was always close in van Zuylen's thoughts when she planned the pristine bedroom. The results of her disciplined approach to the suite of rooms was soothing but dramatic in its monastic ambience. She designed the space to be open and uncluttered, yet private and contemplative.

van Zuylen placed on the garden was crucial to the resulting ambience of her Normandy home.

Gabrielle van Zuylen clearly credited her Paris rooms to Catroux. She credited her own discerning eye, however, to her friendship with the great aesthete Pauline de Rothschild. Years after de Rothschild's death, van Zuylen said, "For me she remains inimitable. Something as simple as a breakfast tray became a work of art when Pauline arranged it—a glimpse of bliss." The sleek van Zuylen residences in France belied the fact that an ancestral medieval castle, Kasteel de Haar in the Netherlands, loomed over the van Zuylen aesthetic. While the castle was an inheritance, the rooms the van Zuylens created with François Catroux evoked a forward-thinking modernity. Gabrielle van Zuylen appreciated just such juxtapositions saying, "The whole key—in clothes, in life—is contrast and variety."

Relying on luxe surfaces and finishes that reflected light, as well as a sense
of timelessness, the Normandy house took on a classic resonance, with modern energy.
Glass walls, polished slate floors, and a teak ceiling defined the sweeping living
room. Gabrielle van Zuylen designed white carpets that delineated the room's seating
areas, and an open fireplace separated them. A large Roberto Matta canvas
hung in the dining area. Design classics—including Mies van de Rohe chairs and a
glamorous brass table by French artist Philippe Hiquily—were used throughout the
space. Hiquily also designed the dining table.

Originally designed in the 1970s, the grand salon in Paris remained virtually unchanged for decades. Modern back-to-back sofas and banquettes were faithful to Catroux's preference for decoration that transcended the era. He set out to create what van Zuylen's friend Pauline de Rothschild referred to as "the pale beauty of a deserted Pacific beach." The effect was a perfect backdrop for van Zuylen's Surrealist paintings and a pair of massive seventeenth-century Venetian mirrors.

LEFT: In Paris, a sleek long gallery with lacquered walls of olive drab showcased the van Zuylen collection of Surrealist canvases and served as a dining space where parties were staged. Exotic floral-skirted tables were set up and paired with Giancarlo Piretti's Plia folding chairs made of Lucite and chrome.

ABOVE: Gabrielle van Zuylen in her Paris petit salon where a massive coromandel screen dominated the room.

Unabashedly feminine and romantic, the prettiness of Gabrielle van Zuylen's Paris bedroom stood in vivid contrast to the grand salon's sleek modernist decoration. Harking back to the late nineteenth century, the room's walls and canopy bed were suffused in a floral print of roses. Cluttered tables held family photographs, flowers, and bibelots.

MONA VON BISMARCK

A Cool Opulence

LIFE BEGAN FOR MONA TRAVIS STRADER (1897–1983) AT THE age of twenty-nine when she married the über-rich Harrison Williams, twenty-four years her senior. Forsaking two failed marriages and a son, the cool Kentucky beauty with startling prematurely silver hair, porcelain skin, and almond-shaped aquamarine eyes had landed the richest man in America. She was hailed as the best-dressed woman in the world during the 1920s and 1930s, wearing her flawless couture wardrobe at the best addresses around the world. With enviable properties—a six-story mansion in New York on Ninety-fourth Street and Fifth Avenue; a Palm Beach estate, Blythedunes; an estate on Long Island, Oak Point; an apartment at the Hôtel Lambert in Paris; and a villa on Capri, Il Fortino—Mrs. Harrison Williams achieved goddess-like stature among the elite. Everything she wore, in addition to what she did and where she went, was recorded in magazines like *Vogue*, *Harper's Bazaar*, and *Town & Country*.

Harrison Williams's 1928 acquisition of the Delano & Aldrich–designed neo-Federal mansion in New York was the perfect venue for the newly minted Mrs. Williams to exercise her powers of captivation. Dinner guest and interior decorator Billy Baldwin called it "one of the most beautiful houses ever built in New York." Ground-breaking designer of the all-white room Syrie Maugham, prompted by Mona Williams's shared fondness for white, deftly conceived the drawing room in silk, brocade, and pale embroidery fabrics. With white walls and masses of white bouquets brought from the greenhouses at Oak Point, the room echoed her own cool beauty, as well as her views on perfection. A Waterford chandelier, blanc de chine porcelain, and crystal were just more refined manifestations of her design aesthetic. There

Mrs. Harrison Williams (later Countess Bismarck) photographed by Horst P. Horst for *Vogue* in 1941, with her dog, a spray of lilies, and her pastel portrait by Henri De Bach.

was nothing typical here, and it was all very fine—and expensive—Mona Williams's measure in all things.

While her New York mansion dazzled, the Long Island mansion, Oak Point, staggered. Even Cecil Beaton was knocked off his feet. In awe of the Hepplewhite and Sheraton antiques, a Bronzino painting, and two Tiepolos, Beaton also noted that a footman supplied him with a gold-plated razor. A series of residences owned by the Williamses in Palm Beach culminated in 1930 with the purchase of a white stucco residence at 513 North County Road. Syrie Maugham was called in to decorate their rooms again, repeating the all-white themes that so suited her client.

Il Fortino, one of the twelve villas Roman emperor Tiberius once owned on the island of Capri, was Mona Williams's next acquisition. In 1936, while cruising the Mediterranean, she fell in love with the abandoned property set on a cliff. Always exhilarated by another decorating project, she sought out Harrison's personal secretary, Eddie von Bismarck, to help sort out the rooms. Count Albrecht "Eddie" von Bismarck-Schönhausen, her future fourth husband, was attuned to her classic style and set about repeating the Syrie Maugham themes she so loved, decorating the drawing room with white silk armchairs and sofas. He brought in eighteenth-century furniture and screens with shell motifs, and added glamorous silver curtains at windows. From the Williamses' Long Island estate, canvases by José María Sert were moved to Capri and installed in the villa's octagonal dining room. A mirrored art deco fireplace ornamented the room, and chain-mail curtains framed the doorways. In Mona's heyday a long glass dining table was in the room's center. A dinner guest recalled how disconcerting it was to eat and see everyone's feet. Glancing over at Mona Williams's slim ankles and custom-made sandals, he then understood the decision. As with all of her rooms, it was the perfect setting for Beaton's "rock crystal goddess." The crowning glory, however, was the gardens, nurtured by Mona for over three decades. Along with plants indigenous to the island, magnolias, echoing her

Cool—like Mona Williams—the drawing room of the Delano & Aldrich house in New York was formally designed by Williams and her decorator Syrie Maugham. Clean and spare, eighteenth-century furniture was the Williams preference. A white color scheme, Maugham's signature, gave the room the requisite glamour that she required. An Isfahan rug in rich shades of blue and orange warmed the room's icy atmosphere, but just barely.

Kentucky roots, were planted; pergolas were amassed with roses; and terraces were carved into the cliffs. Every day, Mona Williams spent hours in the gardens, noted to be the most famous in the Mediterranean and sustained with water brought in by boat from the mainland each day.

A grand apartment in Hôtel Lambert was the Williamses' Paris flat, its rooms once occupied by Voltaire. Later known as Countess von Bismarck upon her fourth marriage (after Williams's death), Mona von Bismarck continued to live at the Hôtel Lambert until she and the ever-accommodating Eddie moved into a grand town house at 34, avenue de New York in 1956. These rooms were

decorated with the help of Jansen designer Stéphane Boudin, while Eddie, known to all the best antique dealers in Paris, acquired paintings for the residence.

Eddie von Bismarck, who died in 1970, provided Mona von Bismarck with her fifth and last husband, Umberto de Martini, Eddie's doctor. Upon de Martini's death, she grew increasingly reclusive. After being photographed for and featured in countless magazines and newspapers, canonized by Cecil Beaton, and noted in a Cole Porter song, Mona Strader Schlesinger Bush Williams von Bismarck de Martini— dressed in Givenchy—retreated from the world until she died at the age of eighty-six in Paris. Her will established the Mona Bismarck Foundation in her Paris home and left Il Fortino to the foundation as a scholarly retreat. Her only child contested the will, and the villa and its contents were sold. Her acolyte Cecil Beaton summed her up best: "Mrs. Harrison Williams possesses the American quality of freshness. No French or South American hostess could possibly have rivalled the almost unreal perfection of crispness and newness she created." She effected the path other American women of wealth would follow, houses in New York, Paris, and Palm Beach, flawless couture from Paris, and photographs in the pages of *Vogue*, yet no one did it quite so well as Mona von Bismarck.

RIGHT: In Cecil Beaton's 1937 painting, Mona and Harrison Williams exuded all the sophistication of their glamorous Syrie Maugham–decorated living room in Palm Beach. Eclectically decorated with English antiques and Jean-Michel Frank tables, the vast room was also furnished with comfortable, low lounge chairs and sofas. The antique chinoiserie paper appeared decades later in the dining room of Pierre Bergé, life and business partner of Yves Saint Laurent.

FOLLOWING SPREAD: Mona's discipline in decoration occasionally gave way to rooms of pure fantasy. One such room was the octagonal summer dining room of her villa in Capri. The Tiepolo-esque murals of acrobats by Spanish artist José María Sert were paired with equally imposing antique silvered mirrors. Sert's style, described as "modern Baroque," was in its heyday when the Williamses commissioned the artist to paint the monumental theatrical scenes for their playhouse at Oak Point on the north shore of New York's Long Island.

OPPOSITE: Mona's view of the Mediterranean from an Italianate grotto chaise in her Capri bathroom. As relayed to her portrait painter Enrico d'Assia, her routine at Il Fortino went as follows: "I sleep till noon, then I go to the sea, then I have to do the flowers."

RIGHT: In the spirit of small, tented French pavilions, an antechamber at Il Fortino was decorated with narrow stripes on the walls and large pink and white stripes on the ceiling, which was replete with trompe-l'oeil tassels. The tented effect was crowned with a fantastical Russian chandelier with a multitude of crystals and tassels. A French gilt grotto-style console was flanked by a pair of Italian Directoire chairs. Henry Clarke photographed the villa after Mona died in 1983; the images were published in the French publication *Connaissance des Arts* in 1987 just before the contents of the villa were sold at auction.

Cecil Beaton extensively photographed Mona for decades. Wearing her favorite
designer, Balenciaga, she posed in the salon of her Parisian residence located in
the Hôtel Lambert. French architect Louis Le Vau designed the mansion in the
seventeenth century, and in the twentieth century it was divided into apartments.
The grand rooms of the Hôtel Lambert were a perfect backdrop for the decoration
schemes she favored and that were set forth by Syrie Maugham in the early 1930s.

PAULINE DE ROTHSCHILD

Disciplined Luxury

"A YOUNG WOMAN MUST BE A DEBUTANTE IN BALTIMORE AND a young married woman in New York City. An old woman must marry a European, preferably in Paris, and live the rest of her life there." This was the pointed witticism that Pauline Fairfax Potter de Rothschild (1908–1976) confided to friend and famed decorator Billy Baldwin. When she decorated a string of stylish rooms in New York, Paris, and London, and at the Château Mouton in France, the worlds of fashion and interior design stopped to take note. Pauline, a distant relation of Diana Vreeland, was a favorite of the 1960s *Vogue* editor. The pair, with the help of Horst P. Horst's camera and Valentine Lawford's prose, made magic. Lawford, whose stories always accompanied Horst's photographs, wrote, "The interior she has created is as revealing of what she is like as are her voice, her features, her gestures, and her clothes," and further defined her intangible style as *"le style Pauline."* In her clothes, she was a Renaissance courtier, wearing tall boots and a jerkin, or the subject of a Watteau painting in flowing robes of silk and slim trousers. In private the iconoclast's strict adherence to the finest—and her ruthless sense of order where editing was essential— were the hallmarks of how she decorated. Through periods of poverty as a child, living with her divorced and alcoholic mother in Paris, Pauline developed her distinctive quest for beauty. At their most destitute, her mother decorated a lone table in their Paris apartment with an extravagant display of white lilies and lilacs. This memory would leave a lifelong imprint on the aesthetic of Pauline de Rothschild.

Her years in New York as a fashion designer at Hattie Carnegie were well chronicled. At her Sutton Place apartment in Manhattan, Pauline insisted on gold-

Baroness Pauline de Rothschild in her bedroom at Grand Mouton, near Bordeaux— a refuge that provided the solitude she yearned for.

leaf moldings in the authentic eighteenth-century style, while dramatically keeping the walls and silk curtains in pure white. She designed a daybed for her bedroom and used taffeta in a pale cerulean blue—a color she would repeat in variations throughout her life. Billy Baldwin, spellbound by these utterly distinctive rooms, marveled at an elusive wall color in the apartment taken from an old, faded Hermès umbrella. Was it a mauve or a gray? Baldwin couldn't say, and Diana Vreeland thought it the color of the inside of a pearl. Indicative of her style, the wall color was highly idiosyncratic— and was, like most of her inspirations, probably derived from a passage in a book, a scrap of fabric, or the color in a painting.

Her apartment in Paris's 14th arrondissement at 13, rue Méchain, with just four rooms and a sort of garden, was exquisitely decorated in *le style Pauline*. She began decorating the eighteenth-century rooms before she married Baron Philippe de Rothschild, her second husband. Even though the baron owned a grand house in Paris, she remained in her apartment throughout their marriage, making arrangements to meet her husband at one of the residences—a particular way of living that allowed her the private hours she craved. The rooms resonated with de Rothschild's innate sense of absolute elegance, along with her shrewd eye for color and a sensual blending of it all. In the *salon vert*, the walls were covered in a Chinese paper of climbing vines and exotic birds, serving as a visual extension of the garden, and long steel-framed sofas with double mattresses were styled after some made for King Gustav III of Sweden. Tables, often holding small vases of her favored irises and shaded silver candlesticks, were placed low. The placement of these and other objects on the floor reflected one of Pauline de Rothschild's favorite decorating devices. In the same room, two eighteenth-century chandeliers, their chains wrapped in green silk, hung off to the far side. In the petit salon, or work room, de Rothschild designed a writing shelf from an old plank edged in silver and tacked ephemera to the walls for inspiration. With her special brand of eclecticism, a Spanish carpet and a pair of antique Jacobean chairs were juxtaposed—classic yet of the moment—while in the oval salon Paul Klee paintings mingled with period Louis XVI furniture and pale pink curtains, which were set off by stone floors.

When she met and married Baron Philippe de Rothschild, Pauline realized the full extent of her design genius. The baron's estate—known as Château Mouton Rothschild, which encompassed vineyards and châteaux in the Médoc region of France—was already famous, but under the care of his baroness, they became

In the Paris bedroom, de Rothschild designed the baldachin bed and, as in the *salon vert*, she covered the walls in an antique Chinese paper. The floor of the room was a simple parquet. She placed an intricately carved Tula metalwork dressing mirror on the floor, which contrasted with the geometric pattern of the flooring. Tula metalwork, named for the Tula armories in Russia, was collected by Russian Empress Catherine the Great. The bedside table was an unusual Russian table of opaline, enamel, and metal. Legendary decorator Billy Baldwin wrote of Pauline, "Her great gift was the unconventional use of conventional things."

legendary. The original château, Petit Mouton, was filled with Second Empire and Victorian decorations, chintzes, and gilt-framed portraits. A second château, carved out of an old farm building, was created on the property and called Grand Mouton—it was Pauline de Rothschild's masterpiece. The library, once a loft, was her masterstroke. Long sofas and an extended chaise, designed by the baroness, were replete with silver legs and layered cushions covered in a brilliant Dresden blue velvet. Slender pillars capped by silver orbs separated the bookshelves, which were carved out of the barn's walls. Pristinely wrapped books on the arts, travel, and gardening predominated her personal section of the library. A reading lamp and a surface for writing under each section were added for taking notes or intense study. A Baroque stairway in stone leading to the château's new rooms was painstakingly constructed in wood before the baroness approved it, after which it was constructed in stone with the balustrade painted in red ocher and pale gray trompe-l'oeil marble.

While there was a rarified air in all of Pauline de Rothschild's homes, her final rooms in London's exclusive residence Albany were pure theater. The main room was decorated by de Rothschild with legendary decorator John Fowler. Capturing the spirit of Tsarist Russia, the parquet floors were painted to imitate marble and scattered with Mongolian goatskins. The dramatic rugs grounded the drawing room's whimsical curtains, designed to be reminiscent of the icicles of a Russian winter, as described in Pauline's *The Irrational Journey*, published in 1966. Her last rooms, as fantastical as the previous ones she had created, were a retreat from reality, perhaps tapping into the memory of her time in Russia when she was far away from the wiles of the world: "Your house helped you escape from a world of snow into one a little less shimmering than the gold, blue, and white outside."

The elegance of Pauline de Rothschild's design aesthetic was nowhere more evident than in the work room of her Paris abode on rue Méchain. A pair of low Louis XVI chairs was intricately detailed in passementerie and placed in front of a simply designed shelf.

In the library of Grand Mouton, a luxuriously elongated chaise and sofa in blue velvet stood in stark contrast to the rough-hewn beams and bookcases. The baroness covered many of her books in white, again creating a contrast to the rustic nature of the room. Valentine Lawford put it succinctly, writing, "The Baroness's rooms have been designed to please herself. So much the better if they should chance also to please others."

LEFT: Pauline de Rothschild was always surrounded by books—
on chairs, tables, and the floor of her bedroom at Grand Mouton.
The baroness designed the iron baldachin bed, made by Jansen,
with naturalistic sapling bedposts. Chinese panels hung on the
walls and were topped with gilded pagoda decorations—one panel
becoming the backdrop for an eighteenth-century cabinet.

ABOVE: De Rothschild's collection of English and Dutch
seventeenth-century silver brushes.

PRECEDING SPREAD: Jeremiah Goodman's illustration of the Grand Mouton living room, called the *grande pièce*.

ABOVE: The baroness assembled an incomparable collection of seventeenth- and eighteenth-century furniture and artwork in Mouton's *grande pièce*. Placed in pairs or alone, for intimate conversation or private contemplation, each chair was meticulously admitted to the room by the baroness and placed for maximum effect. An illustration in an Italian book provided inspiration for the dominant tile floor of blue and red. The chairs, like the collection of modern paintings by masters like Morris Graves, stood as sculpture—with covers chosen to underscore each piece's shape.

RIGHT: The Baron and Baroness Philippe de Rothschild in the grand living room of Mouton.

Fashionably
CHIC

Fashionably Chic women thrive on personal self-expression. Their rooms are filled with oddities and objets d'art from far-flung travels, sophisticated wardrobes, and in some cases their own design work. Their worlds spill gracefully—and quixotically—into the rooms they decorate. Stagecraft is key. Vivid color, the exotic, and the unexpected are used to the maximum in these rooms. They are all collectors, the objects of desire ranging from blue-chip art to whimsical novelties. Never doubting their decorating ability to "make it work," these stylish women do not shy away from the flights of their fertile imaginations. "Mixing it up" is the mantra, of the oh-so-chic Fashionably Chic interior.

BABE PALEY

ELSA SCHIAPARELLI

FLEUR COWLES

PAULINE TRIGÈRE

BABE PALEY

Elegance and Ease

ONE OF "THE FABULOUS CUSHING SISTERS," BARBARA "BABE" Cushing Mortimer Paley (1915–1978) was destined to live in stylish rooms and dress to perfection. Decorator Billy Baldwin, who would go on to work for Babe, said, "Those [Cushing] girls had a kind of monopoly on taste." Babe, with a brief stint as a *Vogue* editor, would catapult to the top echelon of fashion, being named to the International Best-Dressed List over a dozen times and ultimately into the International Best-Dressed Hall of Fame. Often emulated, her faultless looks and innate fashion sense were unique. She created instant trends, but for Babe Paley her style was simply a matter of dressing as she pleased—the true mark of inherent good taste. Perfection was her watchword, yet in her two marriages perfection was an illusion. She threw herself into decorating, fostering her talent through her relationships with the best interior designers of the day. Along with her second husband, CBS mogul William "Bill" Paley, another decorating enthusiast, she sought out the best in all things. With residences in Jamaica and New York (town and country), Babe and the opinionated Bill were always decorating. Her instincts were impeccable, while Bill, the more impressionable one according to the late Albert Hadley, always wanted what he had just seen. "She was the presence," according to Hadley.

Billy Baldwin was responsible for one of the finest twentieth-century American rooms—the Paleys' New York library. The space was transformed from mediocrity, a St. Regis hotel box, into pure fantasy. Here, Babe Paley, in her heyday, and Baldwin were at their most ingenious. Baldwin loved nothing more than using cotton fabric lavishly, and this elegant room was cotton from top to bottom, shirred and

---

Babe Paley had an innate fashion sense as evidenced in her many years on the International Best-Dressed List and in her high-style interiors.

draped. He recognized chic, and this room stood as the ideal backdrop for his client and the couple's lifestyle. So successful was the room, it was later re-created by Baldwin, at the behest of the Paleys, in their apartment on Fifth Avenue. He used the same rug stitched with blackamoor heads and the same Venetian clock chandelier in the room, hanging paintings by Pablo Picasso and Henri Matisse on the shirred cotton walls.

In addition to Baldwin, the Paleys worked with other decorators including McMillen Inc., Sister Parish, Albert Hadley, and Stéphane Boudin of Jansen. Babe got the best out of each one. During her first marriage to Stanley Mortimer, she had carved out an intimate client-decorator relationship with George Stacey. The pair would go off on antique junkets, where she honed her eye—and her taste. Stacey was called in to decorate for the newly married Mrs. Paley. Regardless of the designer, Babe Paley's hand was firmly felt in the final design. She sought out the best—a passion reflected in her impeccable wardrobe and her sublimely decorated rooms.

At the Paley's Fifth Avenue residence, Jansen designer Stéphane Boudin, inspired by Madame de Sévigné's Hôtel Carnavalet, used antique boiseries in the living room, scaling the panels to fit the couple's existing mirrors and paintings. Jansen's director at the time, Paul Manno, described Babe Paley as "one of the few women in the world to have been truly born with a sense of good taste." The bones of the Paley residence were established by Jansen, but the decoration rested with designers Albert Hadley and Sister Parish. Lauded as one of the most elegant rooms in New York, the living room was painted a "taxicab" yellow, as described by designers working for Parish-Hadley at the time. With august French antiques and world-class post-Impressionistic paintings, the room's high-voltage walls pushed an otherwise classic Jansen room to a new level. Chinese lacquered screens flanked a Paul Gauguin painting, and Babe's favorite yellow was splashed on chairs, pillows, and ottomans in three seating areas. Luxurious brown satin sofas offered glamour and Indian cotton prints comfort, while underfoot a dyed goatskin rug sewn into twenty-four-inch squares indulged Babe in her desire for the nonpareil.

For Babe Paley, decorating—and getting the rooms she wanted from her decorator du jour—meant creating environments that never overshadowed but complemented. The resulting rooms were as cultivated and vibrant as the woman who inhabited them. Her favorite decorator, Billy Baldwin, put it most succinctly, saying, "Some people add enormously to a room in a way that no decorator ever could." That was Babe.

OPPOSITE and FOLLOWING SPREAD: For their Fifth Avenue library the Paleys turned to decorator Billy Baldwin to repeat the look that he had previously created at the couple's stunning apartment at the St. Regis hotel. Baldwin wrapped the walls with a shirred brown-and-pink paisley cotton, creating an intimate room that conjured an exotic tent fit for Scheherazade. The Venetian chandelier featured a clock and a pair of frolicking blackamoors. Always favoring French design, the Paleys selected the best French furniture and appointments for this room and the rest of the apartment—yet their rooms never abandoned comfort. The ever soigné Babe Paley insisted on glamour, and this room was a smash— two times over.

LEFT: The entrance hall gallery of the Paleys' Fifth Avenue apartment was free of fuss, letting Pablo Picasso's monumental painting *Boy Leading a Horse* speak to the refined sensibilities of its owners. Bookcases ran the length of the forty-four-foot-long space, planned by Stéphane Boudin of the decorating firm Jansen. Boudin used two patterns of elegant eighteenth-century Italian parquet in the scheme for the floor, thus breaking up the enormously long gallery. Current magazines and art books could always be found on the gallery's large Oriental lacquered tables.

FOLLOWING SPREAD: The color of the Paleys' vibrant yellow Fifth Avenue living room was chosen by Mrs. Paley and the design firm Parish-Hadley. Each of the public rooms of the Paley apartment was as glamorous as the lady herself. George Stacey's stunning brand of decoration had set off Babe Paley to perfection, but as she came into her own, the Stacey grandeur receded to reveal her fresh yet refined aesthetic. This living room was the sum of all that Babe herself personified— polish, sophistication, and legendary style.

While the Fifth Avenue gallery was pristine and the living room ultra chic,
the dining room reflected Babe Paley's unique brand of charm. Parish-Hadley decorated
the walls in a vibrant tree-of-life cotton fabric. The curtains and chairs were
covered in a scaled variation of the print, following a tenet of the French manner of
decorating—employing a single fabric throughout a room.

Fashion photographer John Rawlings captured a perfectly turned-out Babe Paley in 1956. Babe and husband Bill would retreat to Round Hill in Jamaica to recharge, yet never were they far removed from the rich and famous. They were one of many celebrities, stars, and jet-setters that flocked to the enclave of cottages in Montego Bay. Bill Paley built beachfront villa number 26 for Babe, and she set about decorating it in a timeless island style, using woven rattan chairs with colorful cushions and sofas in red. In unassailable Babe style the decoration had rigor, but was relaxed in contrast to her other residences. Her more casual approach here included a standing hat rack where the hats became a part of the decoration. The well-connected fashion executive Boaz Mazor described the Paley place in few words, saying, "It was just perfection."

ELSA SCHIAPARELLI

Shocking Glamour

THE PARIS ROOMS OF FASHION DESIGNER ELSA SCHIAPARELLI (1890–1973), the last she lived in, represented the heady milieu that she had always inhabited. Filled with exemplary pieces from famous artists whom she also called friends, the apartment reflected her decorative aesthetic—an exquisite fusion of the antique and the modern, with her favored Surrealism well represented. The "Queen of Fashion," Italian-born Schiaparelli became fashion's preeminent provocateur in the years before the Second World War. Her name was eponymous with shocking pink, the glorious magenta-pink hue of a bougainvillea. "Shocking," scrawled boldly across a Leonor Fini–designed box in the same color, was the name of her first perfume. Her interiors linger in memory as rooms that reflected her particular brand of style. Much like her tailored suits decorated with giant cicadas and chunky turquoise buttons, her rue de Berri residence was grounded in the classic but always flavored with the provocative.

At the height of her design powers, Schiaparelli moved into the expansive rue de Berri residence, infusing her grand salon with eclecticism and subverting convention. The flat was decorated with advice from the venerable design firm of Jansen as well as her longstanding friend Jean-Michel Frank, father of the modern interior. In the grand salon, just as designer Yves Saint Laurent had described Schiaparelli herself, there was a "bouquet of spells . . . a constellation of the stars . . . a fireworks display, a collection of Surrealist and Cubist art, kaleidoscope colors, provocative palettes of scarlet, lilac and puce." Noted artists, from Christian Bérard and Salvador Dalí to Diego Giacometti and Jean Cocteau, among others, frequented Schiaparelli's salon.

Fashion intellectual Elsa Schiaparelli dressed in her own design, a simple black dress with crocheted collar and gloves with crocheted ruffled cuffs and a looped ribbon turban.

Schiaparelli was at her
zenith during the 1930s. Her
interiors and the clothes she
designed clearly paralleled
each other. In 1938, living
in an apartment on Paris's Left
Bank, the fashion designer
lounged on a diamond-quilted
sofa. The same year a cover
of American *Vogue* featured
an illustration of Schiaparelli's
quilted beach robe.

In her library were strokes of genius—bookcases styled as pagodas and, lining the walls, a suite of three eighteenth-century tapestries by Jean-Joseph Dumons de Tulle, after the sketches of François Boucher for his series Aux Chinoiserie. Here, Madame Schiaparelli emerged in the evenings turned out in a Chinese jacket of cerise satin, as if stepping out of Boucher's tapestried tableau. In later years, her granddaughter Marisa Berenson remembered the addition of a television: "In the evenings when she was at home and she would wear wonderful Chinese costumes or Persian robes with marvellous jewellery, and she'd sit on the sofa she had covered with leopard skin and watch her giant TV, which was perched on a stack of rare 18th-century dictionaries." The decoration here was all "Schiap," the name by which she was known. Venerable designers Jean-Michel Frank and Jansen, often finding themselves managed by their client, were sometimes bewildered by the unorthodox design dictums. Frank, for instance, was dismayed when told that some chinoiserie tapestries styled after Boucher had to be used in the library. Both Frank and Schiaparelli disliked tapestries, but she had found these exceptional and insisted on using them. Her powers of persuasion were such that, intrigued, he painted the space between the tapestries to give the impression that they joined, creating a seamless pattern.

Schiaparelli described her contentment in her autobiography, *Shocking Life*, in regal third person: "This room gives Schiap more joy than any she has lived in. She sometimes makes an appointment with herself to spend the evening alone and do absolutely nothing. She rests with friends who look out smilingly from photograph frames placed on the grand piano, and she is surrounded by beloved paintings put anywhere, on the floor, on chairs, against ancient Chinese bronzes. Then there are books, books, books . . ."

Like most female designers, Schiaparelli was her own best model. In fact, *Vogue* editor Bettina Ballard wrote in her memoir, *In My Fashion*, that for the women who wore Schiaparelli's clothes: "It was like borrowing someone else's chic." Always an original, Elsa Schiaparelli brought her own brand of glamour to her designs, as well as to her inimitable interiors.

Elsa Schiaparelli wrote of her eighteen-room rue de Berri residence in her autobiography *Shocking Life,* "Everything I put in it was lovingly gathered together." The Christian Bérard screen was commissioned for a drafty hall, but Schiaparelli recognized it as a stroke of genius and placed it in the salon. The chimerical screen—depicting the Virgin and her pages and styled as an Italian fresco—was, according to the designer, one of Bérard's greatest works.

"Shocking," the bright pink that was so identified with Schiaparelli, appeared and reappeared throughout the designer's career. Famed photographer Mark Shaw, who so stylishly photographed fashion models and fashionable interiors, posed a model in a Schiaparelli signature-pink evening gown on the Second Empire–style *méridienne-en-confident* in the designer's Paris salon.

ABOVE: Eighteenth-century artist Jean-Joseph Dumons de Tulle designed the three Louis XVI Aubusson tapestries, which were inspired by the Aux Chinoiserie series of François Boucher. Schiaparelli used them as the inspiration for the decoration of the rue de Berri library.

OPPOSITE: Elsa Schiaparelli, in one of her many Chinese jackets, posed for photographer Hans Wild in 1947 in her rue de Berri library, which was animated by the explosive symphony of colors in her eighteenth-century tapestries. Lise Deharme, a Surrealist writer, described Schiaparelli's rue de Berri residence as a house that one falls in love with at first sight.

OPPOSITE: Artist Jeremiah Goodman captured the rich vibrancy of the Schiaparelli library.

ABOVE, LEFT: Cages were repeated motifs in Schiaparelli's fashion collections,
like her "cage" coats made of wire mesh. She kept a pair of pigeons in the tole birdcage
at her Paris house. Jean-Michel Frank designed an oversize birdcage for her Place Vendôme
perfume shop, and her favorite painting was Pablo Picasso's *Oiseaux dans une cage* (*Birds in
a Cage*). All were outward signs of her philosophy of transcendence through fashion.

ABOVE, RIGHT: A fantastic bonewood objet d'art, otherworldly in its bent, resided on
Schiaparelli's library mantel. Her Winter 1938–39 Zodiac collection, celebrating the
solar system, included meteoric, beaded embroideries and starburst capes
inspired by the Neptune fountain at Château de Versailles. Like her Surrealist friends,
Schiaparelli constantly challenged the typical concepts of beauty.

FLEUR COWLES

An Inimitable Flair

FLEUR COWLES (1908–2009), LEGENDARY EDITOR AND WRITER, lived with exuberant flair, and the rooms she decorated reflected her sparkling élan. "I decided [the wing of a bird] would be the symbol of *Flair* [magazine]," she once explained, "because it's flight of fancy, which is what we need if we live an interesting and imaginative life. A flair for something—I don't care what it is, but whatever it is, have elegance in it, even if it's shining shoes. And knowledge—whatever you do, learn more about what you're doing."

Cowles's spirited rooms were never devised by anyone but herself. Her *Flair* was the esoteric magazine (and, at fifty cents a copy, an expensive periodical for the 1950s), where readers got to peek into the worlds of high society, art, literature, and fashion. She is noted as the creator of the modern magazine, and while *Flair* reflected Fleur Cowles's vision for a brief twelve issues, that vision was just the beginning of a life lived to its fullest.

Never lacking confidence, Fleur Cowles claimed, "I invented 'cool.' I remember sitting on the floor and asking my staff, 'If something's hot, isn't it cool?' I said it first." She exhibited the same moxie in how she decorated her residences in New York, London, the English countryside, and Spain.

The petite powerhouse approached rooms like she approached *Flair*. Federico Pallavicini, the designer who brought the magazine's inventive covers to life, said of her New York town house, "She mix all the Louis with all the Georges; Mexican paper flowers with fresh green leaves; Renoir with her own paintings." Pallavicini's description made Cowles's decorating style seem a little all over the place, but for the

The timelessly stylish Fleur Cowles once professed, "The world is a magazine to me. Everything has potential." She used her residences as canvases for an immense talent.

riotously chic Fleur it worked. Her fourth and last marriage to timber executive Tom Montague Meyer set her vision soaring higher, providing her with the money needed to realize interiors that represented her endless creativity.

Cowles with her husband moved to England in 1955, importing her matchless style and patent joie de vivre. In addition to conquering English society, the chic expatriate began restoring a sixteenth-century farmhouse, Great Surries, and a tithe barn on the same property. Built from shipwreck-salvaged timbers and walls of blue-tinted plaster, the barn was stories high. Cowles added expansive light-giving windows, and had galleries built at both ends. She felt strongly about authenticity, but it never kept her from modernizing. The central room of the barn was filled with late seventeenth-century furniture, paintings, sculpture, and rugs from all over the world. Antique handwork was displayed in the room along with a collection of needlework. "I'm a pillow gatherer and I'm an embroidery collector," said Cowles, who was obviously much more than that. Writer Antonia Williams referred to her as a "collector of collections." Her passion was the decorative arts, and she was on the constant lookout for new artists willing to translate her ideas into reality.

In London Fleur and Tom Montague Meyer took up residence at Albany, once the great Georgian manse of Lord Melbourne in Piccadilly. Their elegant set of rooms encompassed the back portion of Albany's first floor. With noted res-

idents spanning centuries, the landmark Albany is still London's foremost address. With two drawing rooms to fill, Cowles swathed Lord Melbourne's ballroom in head-to-toe powder blue. Never one to

LEFT: The inaugural cover of *Flair* in February 1950—like the issues that followed, it was chock-full of the creative and the original. Fleur's passion for the original spilled over into her interiors. She always sought out skilled artisans to execute her original designs for furniture, rugs, and lamps.

OPPOSITE: The barn on an estate in Surrey, England, that Fleur shared with her husband, Tom Montague Meyer, was filled with all things Fleur. A pair of quirky, tiered free-form tables in cinnabar were built around the barn's timbers. Ever inventive, she used pots of scented jasmine for the lamp bases and topped them with red shades. Fleur also designed the patchwork rugs. Friend Wenda Parkinson remarked, "Miss Cowles had a light-hearted touch all her own, a gift for collecting objects of Matisse-like innocent charm and gaiety, for irreverently juxtaposing the pretty and the witty with the rare and the priceless, and producing a result that is not only happy but never, never boring."

148

be a wallflower, she swept through the restoration of these rooms with the same exuberance she exhibited in Surrey. The magnificent ceiling, damaged during London's blitz, was painstakingly restored to its original beauty during a ten-month period. Cowles took up residence at the nearby Ritz to oversee all. It was just the sort of project she loved. Her efforts resulted in what she believed was "the most beautiful drawing room in London." In the second drawing room period Georgian wainscoting was whitewashed, and panels by Pallavicini were installed along one side of the room over a candy-pink-colored banquette. Pallavicini's exotic gold-leaf panels with flower-filled urns were striking and functional, serving as shutters for the windows. A massive stone fireplace and hearth were surrounded by modern-day banquettes, anchoring the room. Cowles's creative eye roamed every corner of the room, and it was filled with her collections and her own works of art.

When Spain beckoned, Fleur Cowles restored and decorated a twelfth-century castle in Trujillo called Las Torres de los Bejaranos. Two of the property's fifteenth-century towers were connected with a new block of rooms—all imbued with her aesthetic genius. As always, she planned the living spaces. Roman arches and stone unearthed from a local site provided most of the bones of the new house and the two towers became bedroom wings. Inside, all the tile, ironwork, and textiles were designed by the indefatigable Cowles. Girls from a nearby village hooked rugs to mimic zebra skins, and Cowles was able to coax nuns at a local convent to embroider hundreds of yards of fabric for the many rooms. Enraptured by the crafts from the surrounding area that she used in the decoration of the house, she helped the local artisans form a collective to sell their work in the United States. Princess Grace had her own bedroom in one of the towers, and noted visitors like Lady Bird Johnson fell under the spell of Las Torres de los Bejaranos—but most likely they had fallen under the spell of Fleur.

The remarkable Fleur Cowles, a twentieth-century original and author of more than sixteen books, said, "I have an idea a second. I'm a born idea myself." She had her deft hand in everything—and it all turned into her unique brand of style. Her godson Lord Rothermere said, "She was a true creature of the renaissance, the sort of great mind that affects and changes the times which it inhabits."

Once a ballroom, the living room at London's Albany was a vision in powder blue.
A vivid painting by Yvonne Mottet was a perfect foil to the room's soft color, and its size grounded Cowles's own effusive works of art that featured flowers and animals.
On either side of the fireplace, Cowles designed bookcases (one can be seen here) that echoed the Georgian period of the building, which had once been owned by Lord Melbourne. In typical Fleur fashion, library steps were used as a table.

LEFT: In 1954, Cowles commissioned Federico Pallavicini to paint a mural of fantastical flowers and trees in decorative urns. Once installed at Fleur's sixteenth-century Surrey estate, the panels were moved to the second of two drawing rooms at her Albany apartment.

ABOVE: Cowles hired famed fashion illustrator René Gruau to work exclusively for her magazine *Flair* in 1950. Never missing an opportunity to hang a painting, Fleur displayed Gruau's portrait of her, in her signature glasses, on a Gothic door of her Albany office.

Stylish and decidedly modern, the main pieces of furniture in Fleur's drawing room in Spain were designed by her and made from local stone with the addition of cushions. A massive stone back-to-back sofa accommodated two bronze free-form tree-shaped lamps. All the rustic chairs and stools were handmade by local artisans. Drawn to the folk-art iconography of the Catholic Church, Cowles hung religious-themed paintings on the walls throughout the estate.

PAULINE TRIGÈRE

Signature Style

PAULINE TRIGÈRE (1908–2002) DESIGNED CLOTHES THAT WERE cut to razor-sharp precision, with an elegant edginess. Likening herself to couturier Madeleine Vionnet, the French-born Trigère disregarded comparisons to the great Coco Chanel: "I think Chanel made ugly clothes, although she used fabric brilliantly." A name long remembered by the most fashionably dressed women of the 1950s, '60s, and the early '70s, Trigère created clothes for women who were sophisticated and always chic. That same Trigère sophistication spilled over into the decoration of her residences—a Park Avenue apartment and La Tortue, a country house in Westchester County, New York.

Trigère designed directly on her models, draping, pinning, and moving elements around until everything was worthy of her discerning eye—and her Park Avenue apartment and La Tortue were given the same Trigère treatment. At La Tortue she moved walls, adding rooms to accommodate her weekend guest list; relocated paintings; constantly changed the display of her collections; and even moved the rocks in the garden outside until they were just so. Pauline Trigère was instantly recognizable by her steely gray coiffure lacquered into submission, bold-as-brass tinted glasses (her trademark), and door-knocker-sized earrings. Her interiors were equally original, evoking Eastern exotica and French sophistication.

While her weekdays in the city were hectic, La Tortue offered tranquility. Throwing herself into her latest projects, Trigère could work—and decorate—away stress. Of the country house's name she said, "Just before I bought the house, I saw three turtles sunning themselves near the pond, and I knew what the house had to be

---

"Fashion is the dictator" was Pauline Trigère's own maxim that governed her approach in work and in the decoration of her rooms.

named." The turtle had already become a part of the Trigère design lexicon. Turtles—made of crystal, silver, porcelain, straw, and stone—seemed to multiply at the Trigère residences; her collection numbering over nine hundred at one count. A signature tortoise print appeared on pillows in cotton and silk, and La Tortue's chatelaine could usually be found lounging about in a matching wardrobe.

While Trigère admitted she often redid things in the country, the primary decoration of her city home remained a constant. When curtains needed redoing, the same fabrics were used. If Trigère found something irresistible, which she often did, it would be integrated into the decoration. A set of Spanish doors—purportedly from a Hapsburg palace and which led to nowhere in her sensuous red sitting room—was just the sort of find that kept Trigère adding to her rooms and collections. Here, splashy graphic needlepoint pillows were piled on the sofa, while in the living room pillows were fashioned from old Japanese silks.

Her rooms reflected Trigère at her most creative. While sometimes veering away from the streamlined approach of her couture into exotic eclecticism, her decorating choices were always very personal decisions. The addition of Louis XV doors, Spanish convent doors, or the Orientalism of her garden room gave her houses a different kind of chic. As in fashion, Trigère's eye for style and elegance were clearly reflected in the rooms she lived in. She believed that "building a wardrobe is like collecting paintings. Your choices should be careful and personal and should reflect your taste, not just for a season, but for years to come." The interiors of Pauline Trigère, like her fashion, were truly personal and infinitely chic.

Pauline Trigère found an antique bed in Paris and adapted it for use as a sofa
in her New York living room. It was rare for her to alter anything in her city apartment,
in opposition to the ever-changing decoration of her country house. She likened
the room's timeless decoration to a closet full of Trigère-designed clothes.
The model's dress was from Trigère's Fall 1988 collection.

Pauline Trigère's preferred
color—a bold red—appeared
in most of her rooms.
Accordingly, she believed that
"when you're feeling blue,
think red." Red felt covered
the walls and the furniture
of her New York study, heating
up the intimate space.

ABOVE: Pauline Trigère used a Clarence House silk print to make feminine curtains and a bedspread, and to line the inside of a built-in armoire in her New York bedroom. She used her favored red on walls and moldings, Roman shades, carpet, and chairs. With its rich color and lavish display of fabric, the room's striking appearance was given over to the classicism that the French-born Trigère so valued.

OPPOSITE: Trigère loved entertaining, and particular attention was given to the decoration of the dining room, in both her city and country residences. In New York the dining table was a reproduction Irish-wake table. Works by Matisse, Picasso, and Modigliani brought her distinctive brand of elegance to sophisticatedly subtle beige walls. Trigère's signature anemones often made their appearance in both houses and on the clothes she designed.

LEFT: Every inch of Trigère's second guest room at La Tortue, the designer's country house in Westchester County, New York, was covered in a signature TRIGERE print. The graphic fabric in black and white was a clever foil to the room's rustic beams and furniture. An antique school bench was placed at the foot of one of the twin beds. Trigère estimated that several hundred yards of fabric were used in the house.

ABOVE: "I'm engaged, married and completely devoted to this house," Trigère declared of her country residence. She added a glass top to the coffee table for the display of her collection of turtles. The sofa was covered in a smart brown chintz scattered with flowers.

FOLLOWING SPREAD: Low tables and ottomans of teak inlaid with mother-of-pearl trees, animals, and flowers helped create an exotic garden room at La Tortue. Trigère's guests would gather for drinks on benches covered in emerald, jonquil, and crimson vinyl that had a silky appearance. In a moment of practicality, Trigère opted for vinyl in deference to her dogs, who had the run of the house. She found that the low furniture worked perfectly with the low ceilings of the old house. The space looked out over the rock garden, conjuring the feel of an exotic Japanese landscape.

Unconventional EYE

The women of the Unconventional Eye are chameleons, with allegiances to no particular style of decorating. Strictly speaking, nothing binds them together— except for their idiosyncrasies. Call them originals. Call them eccentrics. They rebel against such labels, but are without doubt passionate about how they decorate. Expressing themselves through art (their collections, their own works, or their collaborations with other artists), these four women follow one rule— there are no rules. "Whatever the uses of a room, it should be a world unto itself," wrote novelist Edith Wharton, an aesthetic trailblazer who was on a quest for self-expression in the rooms she inhabited. All the women of the Unconventional Eye agree, yet each in her own singular way.

BUNNY MELLON

DOMINIQUE DE MENIL

GEORGIA O'KEEFFE

LESLEY BLANCH

BUNNY MELLON

Graceful Refinement

OF HIS WIFE'S LOVE OF BOTANY AND HORTICULTURE, PAUL Mellon said, "Everything she does in life—her reading, her architecture, her love of pictures—is related in one way or another to this one main interest. To me, that is a very lucky thing for a person to have." Rachel "Bunny" Lambert Mellon (1910–2014), an heiress in her own right, assembled one of the most comprehensive art collections of the twentieth century with her husband, Paul, and accomplished a life of substantial philanthropy while maintaining a surprising level of privacy. It's this discretion, along with her connoisseurship, that will linger long after her possessions have been bought and sold for decades to come.

While wealth afforded Mrs. Mellon the ability to buy anything she wanted, it was her innate ability to fuse disparate design periods, objects, and works of art into an incomparable aesthetic that made her unrivaled among her peers. The list of designers she hired over the years included talents like John Fowler, Billy Baldwin, and Bruce Budd, yet the countless rooms they designed were all stamped with the Bunny Mellon aesthetic. Decorator John Fowler of Colefax and Fowler in London initially instructed Mrs. Mellon by mailed correspondence in the decoration of her New York town house. Two painters, Paul Leonard and William Strom, traveled to London for a crash course in Fowler finishes.

Billy Baldwin, who worked with Mellon for decades, compared her design approach with other clients', saying, "She was the only one who bought the land, took a major role in drafting the architectural plans, supervised the building of the house, designed the gardens and planned every horticultural aspect of them, and then did

Bunny Mellon, with her dog Patrick, in silent contemplation at the Oak Spring Garden Library on her estate in Upperville, Virginia.

the decoration." The Mellons had a four-thousand-acre property, with several houses and stables, in Upperville, Virginia; an elegant Washington town house; a retreat in Cape Cod; a French-style town house in New York; an island house in Antigua; and an apartment in Paris. In each abode, her quiet elegance resonated.

At Oak Spring Farm, the estate in Virginia, architect H. Page Cross created additions in stone to an existing whitewashed log cabin—the result being a rambling house called Little Oak Spring. Despite an oft-stated preference for the visual warmth of wood floors, Mrs. Mellon opted for painted floors in most of her houses. Reminiscent of the geometric stone paving of eighteenth-century Swedish houses, the floors gave instant age and integrity to her rooms. She remained loyal to her colors of choice—blues, whites, and yellows—and her penchant for fabrics in solid colors, simple naturalistic patterns, and the occasional floral chintz. She was known to collect fabrics for later use, often having patterns printed in different colors and on different types of fabric. Her houses and her gardens were her vocation and she took complete control of each and every detail. Baldwin described her decision-making as "electrifyingly efficient." Though she preferred simple fabrics and steered clear of formality, she was ruthless (in the gentlest way) when things didn't turn out precisely as planned. Baldwin said, "Hers is a regime of no tolerance for the mediocre." He devoted pages to her in his autobiography, and of collaborating with Mrs. Mellon he wrote, "She said to me more than once, 'Oh, come on, Billy. Let's take a chance. You aren't sure and neither am I.'" If she wasn't pleased with their efforts she declared, "It didn't work," and they started over.

An award-winning landscape designer, Bunny Mellon had honed her skills from self-study. Her library, a whitewashed modernist building of stone on the Oak Spring property and designed by Edward Larrabee Barnes, reveals the precision to detail Mrs. Mellon maintained. While it's quite charming to find the studied mélange of her beloved collections in the rooms of Little Oak Spring, her library is pristine, and scholarly stringent. The library houses more than thirteen thousand works, many rare, devoted to horticulture and gardening—an unrivaled private collection of rare garden books, botanical prints, and antique manuscripts.

A modern Nicolas de Staël painting *Paysage (Paysage au Lavandou)* in the Oak Spring living room hung with more classical paintings—typical of Mellon's nonchalant decorating aesthetic. Indicative of this nonchalance, she would leave important paintings unframed—propping them on chairs, in bookcases, or on mantels—inviting scrutiny. Her painted Louis XV desk was a cluttered mass of pictures, small paintings, and practicalities.

Along with designing her own gardens at Cape Cod and in Antigua, she redesigned the Rose Garden at the White House during the Kennedy administration. Longtime friends with Jacqueline Kennedy, Bunny Mellon was instrumental in cultivating Mrs. Kennedy's design preferences, and upon completing the design of the White House East Garden after the assassination of President Kennedy, she insisted it be dedicated to her widowed friend. In France she worked with couturier

Hubert de Givenchy on his country-house garden, and was instrumental in restoring the Louis XIV kitchen garden at Versailles. Commenting on the garden at Oak Spring, Mrs. Mellon said, "Nothing should be noticed." Her life and her rooms on the vast bucolic estate were much the same way.

Mrs. Mellon's collection included masterworks by Richard Diebenkorn, Mark Rothko, Camille Pissarro, Pablo Picasso, and several Dutch masters. Her diverse art collection was placed to please the eye, and Mellon's eye was impeccable—one that could roam from a painting by Winslow Homer to a work by Nicolas de Staël and find the beauty in both. Sought out by her peers, Bunny Mellon was emulated and admired for her inimitable style. While grounded in the traditional, her aesthetic veered off into her own distinct brand of bohemianism—one that was patently unique and profound.

LEFT: The peaked garden room of the greenhouse at Oak Spring was topped on the outside with a lead finial designed by jeweler Jean Schlumberger. Inside Fernand Renard's beautiful trompe-l'oeil work on cupboard doors, which conceal storage space, revealed a personal history of Mrs. Mellon in images. Depictions of letters from her children and friends, a poem by husband Paul, gardening paraphernalia, books, fruit, and flowers were all rendered in fine detail, with trompe-l'oeil trelliswork extending above the cabinets to the room's peak. Billy Baldwin spent years searching for the low, oak Louis XV table.

FOLLOWING SPREAD: Mrs. Mellon believed that "a garden, like a library, is a whole made up of separate interests and mysteries." In the Oak Spring Garden Library, a monumental 1954 Mark Rothko canvas glows on whitewashed walls, with small canvases placed like planets revolving around the sun. For drama of scale, Mrs. Mellon displayed a small illustrated book on an easel in front of the large Rothko. Her eye was impeccable at capturing beauty in disparate objects, creating harmony in their placement. Along with her extensive collections, French and Shaker furniture and simple tables crafted on her farm simply adorned the library landscape.

Mrs. Mellon sitting on the library sofa in front of a Diego Giacometti painted bronze table. In the early 1970s, the Mellons commissioned several pieces by Giacometti. The artist agreed to paint the bronzes white, a specific request from Mrs. Mellon. The figurative details and lines of the bronzes were in adherence with Mrs. Mellon's aesthetic for naturalism and simplicity.

ABOVE: Édouard Manet's *George Moore in the Artist's Garden* hung on the
loosely crosshatched walls of lapis lazuli blue in the dining room of the New York
town house. Initially, John Fowler directed the decoration; later Billy Baldwin
designed the Aubusson carpet of scrolling leaves in shades of blue and green.
Painted Louis XVI chairs, curtains on gilt rods, and embroidered linens designed
by Mrs. Mellon created a decidedly Continental mood.

OPPOSITE: The walls of the New York town house anteroom, just outside the living
room, provided a calming contrast to the vibrant dining room walls. Paul Leonard,
who had painted stage sets for Italian director Franco Zeffirelli, was responsible for the
boiserie panels and the whimsical painted tassels below the cornice. Four Giorgio
Morandi still life paintings were hung at different levels over a corner banquette.

OPPOSITE: A detail of Mrs. Mellon's bedroom at the Mellon villa in Antigua, West Indies. In characteristic Mellon style, a grouping of baskets, chair, and stool became a setting of simplicity in concert with a painting of a bird by Balthus. Variations of the simple desk were seen repeatedly in rooms at Oak Spring in Virginia and Osterville, Massachusetts, on Nantucket Sound.

ABOVE: So absolute were her design instincts, Bunny Mellon repeated design elements over and over at her many residences. The canopy bed in her Antigua bedroom was one such piece. She used Porthault's Pansy linens (always Porthault) and a simple butterfly print in navy—the same butterfly print was used at Oak Spring in yellow. She preferred her floors painted, and Paul Leonard executed the octagonal pattern in shades of blue.

DOMINIQUE DE MENIL

Artful Inspiration

AT A 1930 VERSAILLES BALL, IN WHAT DOMINIQUE SCHLUMBERGER de Menil (1908–1997) would later call a chance encounter, she met her husband, Baron Jean de Menil. As a young married couple, another such encounter, with Dominican priest Father Marie-Alain Couturier, would set them on the path that ultimately led to The Menil Collection in Houston, Texas, housing the approximately fifteen thousand objects the couple collected together. Couturier, with a mission to revitalize the art and architecture of the Catholic Church, acquired art from modern masters and commissioned some of the most profoundly spiritual spaces, such as Le Corbusier's chapel in Ronchamp and Henri Matisse's chapel in Vence. His passion inspired the de Menils, and soon the couple began acquiring the world's largest collection of works of art by Surrealist painters Max Ernst and René Magritte, along with works by Georges Braque, Pablo Picasso, and Henri Matisse. Part of the de Menils' daily life, the great paintings were integrated into the intimate settings of their residences in France and in Houston at their Philip Johnson–designed house. Johnson found them "unpretentious, yet arrogant enough. . . . an extraordinary couple. . . . There are some who think they're crazy. I think they're inspired." But at the time, the early 1950s, Houston's upscale neighborhood of River Oaks was stunned. Built in the International Style, the flat-roofed pink brick house sat in unassuming silence, while the city could talk of nothing else.

Today the house still resonates with the de Menil spirit. The collection's one-time director Josef Helfenstein said, "The de Menils were very independent in the way they saw and combined and lived with art. To them it was very spiritual and

Dominique de Menil wearing a skirted suit and sitting on a chaise longue, both by Charles James, in her Philip Johnson–designed Houston house.

intuitive, and that is very palpable in the house today." Raising five children in the now iconic structure and decorating it in a most unlikely style reflected Dominique de Menil's own complex personality. Tall but almost fragile in appearance, she was devout, committed to social reform, and highly intelligent. These attributes merged into a cohesive and worldly decoration of the house under the direction of couturier Charles James. It was another chance encounter—an introduction to Charles James, orchestrated by the de Menils' friend the Duchess of Gramont, Maria Ruspoli—that resulted in James becoming not only Dominique de Menil's favorite dress designer but also the decorator of the Johnson-designed house. Having rejected Johnson's own interior design suggestions, she approached James at the recommendation of her husband, John de Menil ("Jean" had been anglicized). His only decorating project was the de Menil House, and it was a tour de force. James provided Dominique de Menil with the "voluptuousness" she sought and the results were staggering but not without its woes. In an interview she revealed, "Charlie was impossible. But all that mattered was that he was a genius." James approached the house the same way he did his sculptural gowns, shaping and softening Johnson's severe lines, adding vibrant colors for surprise and punctuation. The house seduced, beguiled, and, above all, defied the tenets of interiors of the period.

Color played an important role in the Houston house, much like the striking saffron opera coat lined in ice blue that James had designed for de Menil. Fuchsia and crimson velvets, butterscotch felt, and "Menil gray" defined, delighted, and tempered the severity of Johnson's architecture. Mixing his own paints, James created Menil gray for one wall in the living room. Max Ernst's *Retour de la Belle Jardinière* (*Return of the Beautiful Gardener*) hung on the wall and a heptagonal ottoman designed by Dominique de Menil appeared to float on polished black floors, certainly a Jamesian couture touch. De Menil remembered, "He insisted he could not be inspired to decorate the living room until the black floors were polished till you could see your face in it." The hall doors were covered in bold solid fabrics of fuchsia velvet and pink and ocher felt. She remarked on James's simple principles for the house: "You should only put color on corridors and inside closets. Dark corners and passages were the places for color. The living room should be kept simple."

The stone walls at Pontpoint, the de Menils' château in France, were a striking backdrop for their collection of modern paintings, like Victor Brauner's *Separation d'Irschou*. Dominique de Menil said, "Works of art are like people. They either talk or they're mute. It depends on what surrounds them. They never tell you something if they are in the cold."

For all its seduction, notes of serenity filled the house in much the same way that their French seventeenth-century manor house rooms did. Near Paris, at Pontpoint, the antiquity of the manor's interior materials dominated the decoration with stone walls, exposed wooden beams, and aged red tiles on the floor. Austere Spanish furniture was used here in juxtaposition with the comfortable sofas and the modern art. In the public rooms, neutral colors on

sofas and chairs gave the de Menils' art collection breathing room, while the bedrooms were planned around the coloration of specific paintings.

The Houston house's most significant element was of course the art collection that grew over the years. Beyond the walls of the de Menil House, Dominique de Menil's voice still resonates at the Menil Collection museum, the Rothko Chapel, a museum annex devoted to Cy Twombly, and at a second chapel exhibiting thirteenth-century Cypriot frescoes. Dominique and John de Menil resisted the label "collectors," but she did admit, "My goodness, we did buy a lot." The unprecedented art collection set off by the rooms James had decorated and filled with Baroque and Victorian overtures, framed by Johnson's spare design, made Dominique's house a masterpiece of modern—albeit inhabitable—art.

PRECEDING SPREAD: One of the great strengths of the de Menils' Houston house was its stylishly lived-in look. Beyond the wall—in "Menil gray," a color James hand-mixed specifically for the house—a hall is lined with bookcases, a manifestation of the erudite inhabitants. Dominque de Menil believed that "art is what lifts us above daily life. It makes us more open, more human, more refined, and even more intelligent."

LEFT: Originally designed as a playroom, the dining room was absent of jarring color. Beige tones enhanced the collection of African sculpture. The austere eighteenth-century Spanish furniture stood in contrast to James's sculptural banquette that hugged one side of the room, the shape echoing his body-conscious gowns. Paintings were hung gallery style and included *Music* by Joan Miró and *Oui, oui, oui* by Wols (Alfred Otto Wolfgang Schulze).

OPPOSITE: The smart living-room bar was ingeniously concealed behind a door.
The small space with curved shelves was replete with miniature works of art from the
de Menil collection, colorful glassware, and a few taxidermy birds that
met an unfortunate end against the large glass windows of the house.

ABOVE: The front entry of the Houston house was open and spacious with large settees,
canvases, and sculpture. Tria Giovan photographed the house after an extensive
renovation that was completed in 2004. The preservationists selected a jade silk for the
Venetian settee similar to what Dominique de Menil had found in Paris decades before.

PRECEDING SPREAD, LEFT: As with fashion, Charles James used color to punctuate details, in this case a hallway of doors. His choices of color and his use of Belter furniture provided the dynamic tension the de Menils desired.

PRECEDING SPREAD, RIGHT: Charles James painted the doors in Dominique de Menil's dressing room in various subtle shades of gray. A nineteenth-century chinoiserie games table served as her dressing table, and was juxtaposed with a Victorian chair and a modern dressing stool.

LEFT: Three years in the making, Charles James's butterfly sofa was inspired by Surrealist artist Man Ray's painting *Observatory Time - The Lovers*. Dominique said the sofa "drove upholsterers wild." The upholsterers came and went, with the last one—in a final fitting—getting it right. The subtle play in the sofa's curving lines was present in all of James's sensual evening gowns.

Georgia O'Keeffe

Desert Nirvana

One of the originators of American modernism, Georgia O'Keeffe (1887–1986) found a lifelong canvas for the compelling organic forms she painted amid desert vistas at her beloved Ghost Ranch near the Native American village of Abiquiu, New Mexico. Always an iconoclast, she refused to categorize her work. O'Keeffe—a noted artist in her forties and married to famed photographer Alfred Stieglitz—traveled to New Mexico for the first time in 1929. There she found herself surrounded by the ancient and the austere. Nature beckoned, and she reveled in its offerings.

O'Keeffe settled into Ghost Ranch during the summer months. "As soon as I saw it, I knew I must have it," she said of the little adobe house that she ended up renting. She would maintain her twenty-year marriage by living most of the year in New York with Stieglitz while making summer sojourns to Ghost Ranch. When Stieglitz died in 1946, O'Keeffe left his world forever, and embraced the beauty and inspiration of the desert.

Having long wished to own an eighteenth-century Spanish Colonial compound in the village of Abiquiu, O'Keeffe convinced the owners to sell her the residence she had always wanted. She said, "I bought the place because it had that door in the patio—the one I've painted so often. I had no peace until I bought the house."

O'Keeffe painted what she saw on her daily walks, all the while collecting rocks and whatever treasures she found on the desert floor. Found objects were arranged on plain wooden tables into Zen garden–like compositions. Plant bulbs, sticks, bones, river rocks, and pebbles made up O'Keeffe's assembled still lifes. Art and decoration merged in her desert world. Skulls and flowers (often artificial because the desert

Philippe Halsman photographed Georgia O'Keeffe in 1948 at her ranch in Abiquiu, New Mexico.

terrain yielded so few) were arranged and interpreted on canvas. The few pieces of art hanging on the walls in her New Mexico homes were her own, examples of the phases and shifts that defined her as an artist, and paintings by her mentor, Arthur Wesley Dow, whose tenets encouraged O'Keeffe to "fill a space in a beautiful way."

Extensive work was required to make her Abiquiu village house inhabitable, and after years of renovations, O'Keeffe moved in. The floors of natural adobe were polished and smoothed by local Indian women and covered with animal skins and Native American rugs. Adobe hassocks flanked a glass coffee table and *bancos* (rounded adobe ledges) were used as tables and sofas at the rooms' perimeters. In the living room white canvas cushions topped the *banco*, with pillows in primary red and modern geometrics in red and blue on white animating the otherwise neutral palette. Adobe niches, large and small, along the walls served as reliquaries for O'Keeffe's desert offerings. The artist saw the intrinsic complexities of nature surrounding her home, and they became a part of the decoration inside and out.

Biographer Jeffrey Hogrefe wrote, "Ghost Ranch was Nirvana to O'Keeffe." Her minimalist aesthetic resonating, for the next forty years she would call it home, and in turn, it would provide the kind of physical isolation she needed to paint. Abiquiu, Ghost Ranch, and the surrounding landscape seduced O'Keeffe, and she remained a devoted supplicant until her death in 1986 at the age of ninety-eight.

LEFT: A pair of exterior black doors at Georgia O'Keeffe's ranch in Abiquiu became the subject of a number of her paintings. Photographer Myron Wood photographed the doors during a snowfall.

OPPOSITE: Between the main entrance and the patio, a pair of elk horns illustrated the artist's original decorating aesthetic. A low adobe bench became at once both practical and decorative. The placement of stones alongside a washtub was not random—it was as meticulous as it was meaningful, as were the O'Keeffe canvases that depicted her many rock groupings.

FOLLOWING SPREAD: *Bancos* at the base of the adobe walls were designed for sitting and sleeping. O'Keeffe's *Sky Above Clouds / Yellow Horizon and Clouds* and *Above the Clouds I* hung in stark relief to the plain adobe walls and roughhewn *vigas* (rafters) overhead. In 1965 O'Keeffe allowed a rare glimpse of her rooms at Abiquiu in a story for *House & Garden* magazine. By the 1970s she began changing the colors in the sitting room to natural adobe shades, leaving primary colors behind.

ABOVE: The south windows of the sitting room where O'Keeffe loved to sit. The *banco* was a favorite spot to observe the landscape and the tamarind tree just outside. The artist kept a collection of rocks on the adobe shelf under the window. The rustic *vigas* lent contrast to the crisp primary colors she decorated with at the time.

OPPOSITE: The neutral adobe walls of the sitting room served as a backdrop for an Alexander Calder metal-and-wire hanging mobile. The arrangement suited O'Keeffe's spartan aesthetic and her maxim, "It is only by selection, by elimination, and by emphasis, that we get at the real meaning of things."

OPPOSITE: Eighteenth-century rooms, like this one at Abiquiu, had been used for trading and as sleeping quarters for Native American servants. The Eames chair, colorful Navajo rug, and vibrant pillows brightened the room's austere palette.

ABOVE: O'Keeffe's bedroom had panoramic views with walls of light-giving windows installed during renovations. "Two walls of my room in the Abiquiu house are glass and from one window I see the road toward Espanola, Santa Fe and the world." She often used the road as a subject for her paintings. In contrast to the natural walls, black patent-leather curtains hung at the windows. To the wall alongside the fireplace, O'Keeffe affixed a sculptural hand of Buddha in the mudra pose, meaning "Fear not."

LESLEY BLANCH

Nomadic Romanticism

ENGLISH AUTHOR AND HISTORIAN LESLEY BLANCH (1904–2007) could have easily been mistaken for one of the heroines she wrote about during her journey-filled life. Like her protagonists, the alluring Blanch was the epitome of the quixotic romantic bohemian who leaves a sheltered life for one in foreign climes, swathed in robes of silk and brocade. Lesley Blanch was anything but the typical English rose. She grew up during the Edwardian era and, as a child, was always attracted to the Romantic and mad for all things Russian, longing to travel to "the wilder shores of love"—which became the title of her first book, published in 1954. Never out of print, the book profiles four of Lesley's favorite nineteenth-century women whose lives led them to explore the exotic East.

The central figure in Lesley's childhood and as a young woman was a mysterious Russian émigré she called "the Traveler" (she often referred to him in her books yet never revealed his name). Coming in and out of her life, bringing unusual and sometimes inappropriate gifts, he believed that "things are loyal. They remain when people go." This would be Lesley Blanch's modus operandi for how she lived, and how she decorated.

Integral to her acquisitions was her affinity to particular pieces. Blanch wrote extensively about her design aesthetic, and there are countless pearls of wisdom she left for fellow travelers. "From an early age I collected things—objects rather than objets d'art, and took them about with me, even on the shortest journeys. I have never understood the dictum always travel light." Her homes (she moved many times) were caravans; her possessions, a moveable trove of the precious and the beloved: rugs,

Adventure seeker Lesley Blanch, shown at Petra in Jordan, described her approach to decorating: "My rooms are gestures of defiance against every rule of the pundit decorators."

"Surround oneself with the things you love and your house will make you happy; I never decorate, I just make sure that I'm going to be comfortable and let the effect come with the living." Always ready with a sage maxim, author Lesley Blanch was the epitome of the wandering bohemian. Not too far from her house in Menton, France, she had a getaway—once a donkey stable—where she would go to write.

prayer mats, cushions of all sorts (her own needlework), textiles, and her objects, which included Russian icons, samovars, and books.

When Henry Clarke photographed her for *House & Garden* in 1974, Lesley Blanch was settled into a neat house in Menton, France, on the Mediterranean. Here she would laze about on divans and a raised dais, where a rare icon found in Istanbul was framed by a hanging Persian rug that was mounted on the wall. Usually adorned in eighteenth-century caftans, rough-cut stone jewelry, and dramatic turbans, Blanch became part of the decoration, often matching the color of her wardrobe to a particular room. Her pillows, with stitched scenes from her travels and depictions of her interests, were scattered about on rugs and sofas. "My cushions are so many magic carpets transporting me back to faraway places I have known and loved and now re-create in terms of gros-point," she wrote. "As I stitch, they come to life again, and I am once more in the dappled shadow of Aleppo's souks, in the Pachmakli along the road in Turkestan, or on a rooftop in Delhi . . . Ah! Needlework thy name is nostalgia!"

Like Lady Jane Digby, one of the subjects in *The Wilder Shores of Love*, as a romantic Lesley Blanch was seduced by the East. Her eclectic rooms and collections were the result of those fabled far-flung travels. With her peripatetic lifestyle, Blanch likened herself to a snail (carrying her most precious possessions on her back); she was unchanging nevertheless in the decoration of her rooms. Feeling quite at home anywhere, she emphasized atmosphere over décor—an atmosphere infused with the intoxicating scent of jasmine and the exotic aura of Lesley Blanch herself.

With a mountainous number of pillows, some of her own design in gros-point, and layer upon layer of rugs, Blanch created a corner in her Mediterranean living room for relaxing near the fireplace. Blanch said, "You must have comfort first. Everything else follows naturally." She designed the conical fireplace hood after a Turkish one.

ABOVE: Lesley Blanch's great friend Henry Clarke photographed her many times. He caught up with her in Paris, photographing her for American *Vogue* in 1966. She posed wearing a Syrian robe, trimmed in gold passementerie, over a long tunic.

RIGHT: Like a colorful caravan, the living room worktable was piled high with papers and baskets—her yarns and her research close at hand. Blanch would not have dreamed of tidying it up, preferring it that way. Russian icons, paintings, and photographs hung close by, above simple bookcases chock-tull ot reading material. She labeled the objects she found and those that were given to her—noting an item's meaning and origin.

LEFT: Stuccoed walls enclosed another comfortable seating arrangement in a rustic little getaway in Menton, France. Blanch's nomadic existence led her to create instant ambience anywhere, with a few pillows and rugs.

ABOVE: Blanch surrounded herself with plants wherever she lived. Her Mediterranean terrace was sheltered by bamboo, jacaranda, fig, and jasmine. A lace-covered table with iron chairs from France provided the setting for an alfresco luncheon—carafes topped with lemons as stoppers and a small bouquet of flowers in a goblet.

BIBLIOGRAPHY

LESLEY BLANCH

Blanch, Lesley. *Journey into the Mind's Eye.* London: Collins, 1968.

———. "The Joys of Comfort." *Architectural Digest,* April 1985, 34, 38, 40, 42.

———. *The Wilder Shores of Love.* London: John Murray, 1954.

Blanch, Lesley, and Georgia de Chamberet, ed. *On the Wilder Shores of Love: A Bohemian Life.* London: Virago Press, 2015.

Boston, Anne. *Lesley Blanch: Inner Landscape, Wilder Shores.* London: John Murray, 2010.

Cleave, Maureen. "A Mystery Woman Lifts the Veil: A Vivid Imagination Has Sustained Author Lesley Blanch throughout Her Long Life." *Daily Telegraph*, September 1981. Accessed February 16, 2015. http://www.lesleyblanch.com/popups /dailytelegraphlesleyblanch.html.

Fayard, Judy. "Lesley Blanch: Fiercely Determined Romantic." *W* magazine, October 1976. Accessed February 16, 2015. http://www.lesleyblanch.com /popups/wmagazinelesleyblanch.html.

Guppy, Shusha. *Looking Back: A Panoramic View of a Literary Age by the Grandes Dames of European Letters.* Latham, New York: British American Publishing Ltd., 1991.

"The Romantic Rooms Lesley Blanch Has Created with Treasures from a Lifetime of Travel." *House & Garden,* April 1974, 96–101.

Salmon, Alice Wooledge. "Wilder Shores of Eating." *House & Garden,* February 1991. Accessed February 16, 2015. http://www.lesleyblanch.com/popups /housegardenlesleyblanch.html.

Wade, Valerie. "Chez Elles: Lesley Blanch, Nancy Mitford and Mary McCarthy Are Three Successful Women Writers Living in Paris." *Sunday Times Magazine*, September 1969. Accessed February 16, 2015. http://www.lesleyblanch.com/popups /sundaytimeslesleyblanch.html.

EVANGELINE BRUCE

Barron, James. "Evangeline Bruce, 77, Hostess Known for Washington Soirees." *New York Times,* December 14, 1995. Accessed June 10, 2015. http://www.nytimes. com/1995/12/14/us/evangeline-bruce-77-hostess -known-for-washington-soirees.html.

Beaton, Cecil. "The Amazing Bruces." *Vogue,* September 15, 1964, 122–27.

Beevor, Antony, and Artemis Cooper. "Obituary: Evangeline Bruce." *Independent*, December 14, 1995. Accessed June 10, 2015. http://www.independent.co.uk/news /people/obituary-evangeline-bruce-1525799.html.

"The Bruce Touch." *Vogue,* June 1, 1968, 164–67.

Coleridge, Nicholas. *The Fashion Conspiracy.* New York: Random House, 2012.

Conroy, Sarah Booth. "Doyenne of Elegance: Evangeline Bruce, in a Class by Herself." *Washington Post,* December 14, 1995. Accessed June 12, 2015. https:// www.washingtonpost.com/archive/lifestyle/1995/12/14 /doyenne-of-elegance/9276d92f-50aa-4dff-8b69 -fcb676bf2ed0/.

de Rothschild, Pauline. "Evangeline Bruce: Her Listening Gaiety." *Vogue,* September 15, 1964, 128, 192.

Jones, Chester. *Colefax and Fowler: The Best in English Interior Decoration.* London: Barrie and Jenkins, 1989.

Owens, Mitchell. "At Home with: Evangeline Bruce; the Improbable Author." *New York Times,* March 16, 1995. Accessed June 10, 2015. http://www.nytimes. com/1995/03/16/garden/at-home-with-evangeline -bruce-the-improbable-author.html.

Plumb, Barbara. *Horst Interiors.* New York: Bulfinch Press, 1991.

Schlesinger, Jr., Arthur. "Evangeline Bruce in London." *Architectural Digest,* March 1991, 164–69.

Wood, Martin. John Fowler: *Prince of Decorators.* London: Francis Lincoln Ltd., 2007.

SYBIL CONNOLLY

Adam, James. *The Sybil Connolly Collection.* London: Bonhams, 1998.

"Architectural Digest Visits Sybil Connolly." *Architectural Digest,* December 1973, 58–63.

Bryant, Kathy. "A Pattern for Success." *Los Angeles Times,* June 15, 1996. Accessed November 6, 2015. http:// articles.latimes.com/1996-06-15/home/hm-15574_1 _sybil-connolly.

Connolly, Sybil. "Charm and Personality in Design."*Architectural Digest,* September 1978, 38.

———. *In an Irish House.* London: Weidenfeld and Nicholson, 1988.

———. *Irish Hands: The Tradition of Beautiful Crafts.* New York: Hearst Books, 1994.

Connolly, Sybil, and Helen Dillon. *In an Irish Garden.* London: Weidenfeld and Nicholson, 1986.

"Enterprise in Old Erin: The Irish Are Making a Stylish Entrance into the World of Fashion." *Life,* August 10, 1953, 46–50.

Nemy, Enid. "Sybil Connolly, 77, Irish Designer Who Dressed Jacqueline Kennedy." *New York Times,* May 8, 1998. Accessed November 6, 2015. http://www.nytimes .com/1998/05/08/arts/sybil-connolly-77-irish-designer -who-dressed-jacqueline-kennedy.html.

O'Byrne, Robert. "The Mink and Diamonds of Irish Fashion: Sybil Connolly." *Irish Arts Review Yearbook* 16 (2000).

Rosenberg, Karen. "A Shower of Tiny Petals in a Marriage of Art and Botany." *New York Times,* October 22, 2009. Accessed November 7, 2015. http://www.nytimes .com/2009/10/23/arts/design/23delany.html.

Wilson, Jose, and Arthur Leaman. "Ireland." *House & Garden,* April 1961, 146.

LADY DIANA COOPER

Beaton, Cecil. "Lady Diana Cooper's One-Woman Farm." *Vogue,* September 1, 1941, 62–63, 136.

_____. *The Glass of Fashion.* London: Weidenfeld and Nicholson, 1954.

"The Charming Eighteenth Century Style of Lady Diana Cooper." *Vogue,* June 1, 1923.

Cooper, Artemis. *The Diana Cooper Scrapbook.* London: Hamish Hamilton, 1987.

Cooper, Diana. *The Light of Common Day.* London: Rupert Hart-Davis, 1959.

_____. *The Rainbow Comes and Goes.* London: Rupert Hart-Davis, 1958.

_____. *Trumpets from the Steep.* London: Rupert Hart-Davis, 1960.

Knox, Tim, and Francis Hammond. *The British Ambassador's Residence in Paris.* Paris: Flammarion, 2011.

Lees-Milne, Alvilde. *The English Woman's House.* London: Breslich & Foss, 1984.

Peck, Michael. *The English Room.* London: Weidenfeld and Nicholson, 1985.

"Playful Clues to Remarkable Lives." Christie's, April 6, 2016. Accessed July 10, 2016. http://www.christies.com /features/Martin-Battersby-murals-for-Duff-and-Lady -Diana-Cooper-7212-1.aspx.

Shusa, Guppy. *Looking Back.* Latham, New York: British American Publishing Ltd., 1991.

Whistler, Laurence. *The Laughter and the Urn: The Life of Rex Whistler.* London: Weidenfeld and Nicholson, 1985.

Ziegler, Philip. *Diana Cooper.* London: Hamish Hamilton, 1981.

FLEUR COWLES

Collins, Amy Fine. "A *Flair* for Living." *Vanity Fair,* June 9, 2009. Accessed May 7, 2015. http://www.vanityfair .com/magazine/1996/10/fleur-cowles199610.

Cowles, Fleur. *She Made Friends and Kept Them.* New York: Harper Collins, 1996.

de Ocampo, Brooke, with Elizabeth Gage. *Bright Young Things: London.* New York: Assouline, 2002.

MacIsaac, Heather Smith. "Editor in Chic: At Home in London with Fleur Cowles, the World's Most Urbane Woman." *New York Times Magazine,* July 6, 2003, 40–46.

Nemy, Enid. "Fleur Cowles, 101, Is Dead; Friend of the Elite and the Editor of a Magazine for Them." *New York Times,* June 8, 2009. Accessed May 7, 2015. http://www.nytimes .com/2009/06/08/business/media/08cowles.html.

Vincent, David. "Fleur Power." *Town & Country,* February 2010, 76–81, 111.

Williams, Antonia. "Fleur Cowles and Her Marvelous Barn of a Place." *British Vogue,* October 1, 1971, 152–55.

DOMINIQUE DE MENIL

Bernier, Georges, and Rosamond Bernier, eds. *The Best in European Decoration.* New York: Reynal & Company, 1963.

Bernier, Rosamond. "A Gift of Vision: On the Opening of Her New Museum, Dominique de Menil Reflects on the Houston House Where It All Began." *House & Garden,* July 1987, 120–29, 180–82.

Claridge, Laurann, Holly Moore, and Rob Brinkley. *Domestic Art: Curated Interiors.* New York: Assouline, 2008.

Filler, Martin. "The Real Menil." *The Magazine Antiques,* September 2008, 78–85.

Gere, Charlotte, and Marina Vaizey. *Great Women Collectors.* London: Philip Wilson Publishers, 1999.

Glueck, Grace. "The de Menil Family: The Medici of Modern Art." *New York Times,* May 18, 1986. Accessed March 23, 2015. http://www.nytimes.com/1986/05/18 /magazine/the-de-menil-family-the-medici-of -modern-art.html.

Goodman, Wendy. "The Chosen One." *New York Magazine,* July 24, 2014. Accessed March 20, 2015. http://nymag .com/nymag/strategist/designhunting/menil -house-2014-7/.

Helfenstein, Josef and Laureen Schipsi. *Art and Activism: Project of John and Dominique de Menil.* Houston: Menil Collection, 2010.

Middleton, William. "A House that Rattled Texas Windows." *New York Times,* June 3, 2004. Accessed March 23, 2015. http://www.nytimes.com/2004/06/03/garden/a-house -that-rattled-texas-windows.html.

Viladas, Pilar. "Style; They Did It Their Way." *New York Times Magazine,* October 10, 1999. Accessed March 23, 2015. http://www.nytimes.com/1999/10/10/magazine /style-they-did-it-their-way.html.

PAULINE DE ROTHSCHILD

Baldwin, Billy, with Michael Gardine. *Billy Baldwin: An Autobiography.* New York: Little, Brown and Company, 1985.

"Baron and Baroness de Rothschild at Petit Mouton." *Vogue,* February 15, 1956, 100–101.

Bradshaw, George. "Baltimore Hostesses." *Vogue,* November 15, 1972, 130–33.

de Rothschild, Pauline. *The Irrational Journey.* London: Hamish Hamilton, 1968.

_____. "The Irrational Voyage: Notes on Leningrad." *Vogue,* October 15, 1966, 142–44, 167–71.

"Hostess with the Mostest." *The World of Interiors,* November 2014, 158–65.

Jones, Chester. *Colefax & Fowler: The Best in English Interior Decoration.* London: Barrie and Jenkins, 1989.

Ladd, Mary-Sargent. *The French Woman's Bedroom.* New York: Doubleday, 1991.

Lawford, Valentine. *Horst: His Work and His World.* New York: Alfred A Knopf, 1984.

_____. "Le Style Pauline." *Vogue,* June 1, 1969, 151–53, 159–60.

_____. "Power of Dreams." *Vogue,* July 1, 1963, 87–97, 103–5.

Lawford, Valentine, and Horst P. Horst. *Vogue's Book of Houses, Gardens, People.* New York: The Viking Press. 1968.

Owen, Mitchell. "Pauline on My Mind." *New York Times Magazine,* Fall 2000, 154–62.

Plumb, Barbara. Horst Interiors. Boston: Bullfinch Press, 1993.

Tapert, Annette, and Diana Edkins. *The Power of Style: The Women Who Defined the Art of Living Well.* New York: Crown Publishers, 1994.

"Vie de Chateau . . . Glimpses of a Romantic Woman." *Vogue,* December 1, 1963, 106–7.

LOUISE DE VILMORIN

Beaton, Cecil. *The Glass of Fashion.* London: Weidenfeld and Nicholson, 1954.

de Vilmorin, Louise. "Sous le charme de notre Verrieres." *Connaissance des Arts,* September 1959, 70–75.

Douglas, Murray, and Chippy Irvine. *Brunschwig & Fils Style.* New York: Bulfinch Press, 1995.

Hanoteau, Guillaume. "Avec madame de . . . Louise de Vilmorin." *Paris Match,* n.d., 14, 59.

Ladd, Mary-Sargent. *The French Woman's Bedroom.* New York: Doubleday, 1991.

Lyon, Ninette. "Second Fame." *Vogue,* July 1, 1965, 122–23.

McCabe, Marilyn. "The Words Were Said: Poems by Louise Lévêque de Vilmorin – Translated by Marilyn McCabe." *Numéro Cinq III,* no. 7 (July 2012). Accessed May 9, 2014. http://numerocinqmagazine.com/2012/07/01/the-words-were-said-poems-by-louise-leveque-de-vilmorin-translated-by-marilyn-mccabe/.

Petkanas, Christopher. "Chichi Devil." *T: The New York Times Style Magazine,* February 19, 2009. Accessed May 11, 2014. http://www.nytimes.com/2009/02/22/style/tmagazine/22vilmorin.html.

Prioleau, Betsy. *Seductress: Women Who Ravished the World and Their Lost Art of Love.* New York: Viking Penguin, 2003.

"Q & A: Stylemaker Murray Bartlett Douglas, Retired Vice-Chairman of Brunschwig & Fils." *Cincinnati,* October 1995, 102. Accessed May 9, 2014. https://books.google.com/books?id=2QsDAAAAMBAJ&pg=PA102&lpg=PA102&dq=murray+douglas+Verrieres+brunschwig+and+fils&source=bl&ots=o53a7w3NrI&sig=VlVq-3b4BsyDjSsmOhgOJKNuG9E&hl=en&sa=X&ei=IF9GVdH8CcGeggSd9YGQBw&ved=0CDoQ6AEwBA#v=onepage&q=murray%20douglas%20Verrieres%20brunschwig%20and%20fils&f=false.

Ziegler, Philip. *Diana Cooper.* London: Hamish Hamilton, 1981.

BUNNY MELLON

Baldwin, Billy. *Billy Baldwin Decorates: A Book of Practical Decorating Ideas.* New York: Holt, Rinehart and Winston, 1972.

_____. *Billy Baldwin Remembers.* New York: Harcourt Brace Jovanovich, 1974.

Baldwin, Billy, with Michael Gardine. *Billy Baldwin: An Autobiography.* New York: Little, Brown and Company, 1985.

Bartlett, Apple Parish, and Susan Bartlett Crater. *Sister Parish: The Life of the Legendary American Interior Designer.* New York: The Vendome Press, 2000.

Lewis, Adam. *Billy Baldwin: The Great American Decorator.* New York: Rizzoli, 2010.

Mellon, Bunny. "Green Flowers and Herb Trees." *Vogue,* January 1, 1965, 208–11.

Moss, Charlotte. "The Eloquence of Silence." *T: The New York Times Style Magazine,* June 15, 2014, M298.

Property from the Collection of Mrs. Paul Mellon: Interiors Sessions 1–2. New York: Sotheby's, 2014.

Property from the Collection of Mrs. Paul Mellon: Interiors Sessions 3–5. New York: Sotheby's, 2014.

GEORGIA O'KEEFFE

"Five Famous Artists in their Personal Backgrounds." *House & Garden,* December 1965, 176–77.

Hogrefe, Jeffrey. *O'Keeffe: The Life of an American Legend.* London: Bantam Press, 1992.

Lynes, Barbara Buhler. *Georgia O'Keeffe and Her House.* Georgia O'Keeffe Museum. Film. 1997.

Lynes, Barbara Buhler, and Agapita Judy Lopez. *Georgia O'Keeffe and Her Houses: Ghost Ranch and Abiquiu.* New York: Harry N. Abrams, 2012.

Patten, Christine Taylor. *O'Keeffe at Abiquiu.* New York: Harry N. Abrams, 1995.

BABE PALEY

Abbott, James Archer. *Jansen.* New York: Acanthus Press, 2006.

Baldwin, Billy, with Michael Gardine. *Billy Baldwin: An Autobiography.* New York: Little, Brown and Company, 1985.

Bartlett, Apple Parish, and Susan Bartlett Crater. *Sister Parish: The Life of the Legendary American Interior Designer.* New York: The Vendome Press, 2000.

Footer, Maureen. *George Stacey and the Creation of American Chic.* New York: Rizzoli, 2014.

Grafton, David. *The Sisters: The Lives and Times of the Fabulous Cushing Sisters.* New York: Villard Books, 1992.

"Jamaica: High Society's Giddy Days at the Hill." *The Telegraph,* November 13, 2000. Accessed September 8, 2016. http://www.telegraph.co.uk/travel/destinations/centralamericaandcaribbean/jamaica/722930/Jamaica-High-societys-giddy-days-at-the-Hill.html.

Lewis, Adam. *Billy Baldwin: The Great American Decorator.* New York: Rizzoli, 2010.

Parish, Sister, Albert Hadley, and Christopher Petkanas. *Parish-Hadley: Sixty Years of American Design.* New York: Little, Brown and Company, 1995.

Prisant, Carol. "Babe & I." *Town & Country*, December 2010, 152–56.

Tapert, Annette, and Diana Edkins. *The Power of Style: The Women Who Defined the Art of Living Well.* New York: Crown Publishers, 1994.

Tweed, Katharine, ed. *The Finest Rooms by America's Great Decorators.* New York: The Viking Press, New York.

Wood, Martin. *Sister Parish: American Style.* London: Francis Lincoln Ltd., 2011.

HÉLÈNE ROCHAS

Aillaud, Charlotte. "Architectural Digest Visits: Hélèn Rochas." *Architectural Digest,* April 1984, 126–33, 188–90.

"At Home in the Sky: Hélène Rochas' New York Retreat." *Vogue,* October 1979, 356–59.

Collection Hélène Rochas. Paris: Christie's Paris, September 27, 2012.

de la Renta, Françoise. "The Irresistible Life." *Vogue,* August 1976, 147–49.

Petkanas, Christopher. "Fabulous Dead People: Hélène Rochas." *W* magazine, September 2012. Accessed June 19, 2016. http://www.wmagazine.com/culture /art-and-design/2012/09/helene-rochas-christies -estate-auction/.

"Rue Barbet de Jouy chez M. et Mme Marcel Rochas." *Plaisir de France,* November 1948, 44–48.

ELSA SCHIAPARELLI

Baudot, François. *Fashion Memoir: Elsa Schiaparelli.* London: Thames and Hudson, 1997.

Berenson, Marisa. *Elsa Schiaparelli's Private Album.* London: Double-Barrelled Books, 2014.

Blum, Dilys E. *Shocking! The Art and Fashion of Elsa Schiaparelli.* New Haven: Yale University Press, 2003.

Collection personnelle d'Elsa Schiaparelli. Paris: Christie's Paris, 2014.

Menkes, Suzy. "Celebrating Elsa Schiaparelli." *New York Times,* November 18, 2013. Accessed May 5, 2015. http://www.nytimes.com/2013/11/19/fashion /Celebrating-Elsa-Schiaparelli.html.

Schiaparelli, Elsa. *Shocking Life: The Autobiography of Elsa Schiaparelli.* London: J. M. Dent & Sons Ltd., 1954.

PAULINE TRIGÈRE

Collins, Amy Fine. "Every Inch an Original." *Vanity Fair,* December 1999, 344–47, 367–69.

Felder, Deborah G., and Diana Rosen. *Fifty Jewish Women Who Changed the World.* New York: Citadel, 2003.

Goodman, Wendy. "Living with Style: Pauline Trigère." *House & Garden,* July 1991, 42.

Greene, Gael. "The Style of Pauline Trigère: Enduring Qualities Enliven Her New York Residence." *Architectural Digest,* September 1988, 190–95.

Herman-Cohen, Valli. "Pauline Trigère, 93; Fashion Designer Bridged Cultures." *Los Angeles Times,* February 15, 2002. Accessed June 2, 2015. http://articles.latimes.com/2002 /feb/15/local/me-trigere15.

Morris, Bernadine. *The Fashion Makers: An Inside Look at America's Leading Designers.* New York: Random House, 1978.

Nemy, Enid. "Chez Trigère, Turtles Prevail and Trees Beckon." *New York Times,* October 8, 1992. Accessed June 2, 2015. http://www.nytimes.com/1992/10/08/garden /chez-trigere-turtles-prevail-and-trees-beckon.html.

"Pauline Trigère: The Fashion Designer's Country House La Tortue." *Architectural Digest,* March/April 1974, 70–75.

Petkanas, Christopher. "Pauline Trigère." *Fabulous Dead People* (blog). T: The New York Times Style Magazine, February 28, 2011. Accessed June 2, 2015. http:// tmagazine.blogs.nytimes.com/2011/02/28/fabulous -dead-people-pauline-trigere/.

GABRIELLE VAN ZUYLEN

Aillaud, Charlotte. "In Art's Sway: Baroness van Zuylen's Paris Residence." *Architectural Digest,* December 1985, 172–77.

"Deco 1975: Masterminded by François Catroux, a New International Style." *Vogue,* March 1975, 138–39.

Ladd, Mary-Sargent. *The French Woman's Bedroom.* New York: Doubleday, 1991.

Lawford, Valentine. "Life at Full Fling: Baron and Baronne Thierry van Zuylen." *Vogue,* August 15, 1970, 124–29.

"Personal Style: Baronne Thierry van Zuylen." *Vogue,* March 1, 1972, 84–85.

van Zuylen, Gabrielle, and Marina Schinz. *The Gardens of Russell Page.* New York: Stewart, Tabori & Chang, 1991.

MONA VON BISMARCK

Beaton, Cecil. *The Glass of Fashion.* London: Weidenfeld and Nicholson, 1954.

"Beauty—Continuing: Countess Bismarck." *Vogue,* July 1, 1959, 74–77.

Birchfield, James. *Kentucky Countess: Mona Bismarck in Art & Fashion.* Lexington, Kentucky: University of Kentucky Publishing Services, 1997.

"Country Living in the U.S.A.: Oak Point." *House & Garden,* June 1949, 82–85.

de Gaigneron, Axelle. "Que deviendra Le Fortino?" *Connaissance des Arts,* November 1965, 92–101.

Lawford, Valentine. "A Garden of the Heart: Countess Bismarck's Triumph of Work and Imagination on Capri." *Vogue,* April 1, 1967, 182–87, 203–05.

Metcalf, Pauline. *Syrie Maugham.* New York: Acanthus Press, 2010.

"Mrs. Harrison Williams." *Vogue.* November 1, 1941, 71.

"Mrs. Harrison Williams: Wardrobe Schemes." *Vogue,* February 15, 1948, 80–83.

Tapert, Annette, and Diana Edkins. *The Power of Style: The Women Who Defined the Art of Living Well.* New York: Crown Publishers, 1994.

Weaver, William. "Mona Bismarck on Capri: The Last Images of Il Fortino." *Architectural Digest,* February 1989, 32, 36, 43.

Wright, Richardson Little, ed. *House & Garden's Complete Guide to Interior Decoration.* New York: Simon & Schuster, 1942.

IMAGE CREDITS